"Rich Mouw's reflection on Christian faith, pa͟ essential reading for our times from one of the wisest and kindest voices around."

John Inazu, Sally D. Danforth Distinguished Professor of Law and Religion at Washington University in St. Louis

"As I read *How to Be a Patriotic Christian*, one word kept coming to me: *wisdom*. Our civic life requires wisdom, and this book by Richard Mouw helps to supply it page after page. The balance in this book and its tone help show the way to be a good loving Christian and a good citizen at the same time. May their tribe thrive and increase."

Darrell Bock, senior research professor of New Testament studies and executive director for cultural engagement at the Hendricks Center, Dallas Theological Seminary

"This is no 'how-to-be-a patriotic-Christian' self-help book; rather, this book provides us with wise Mouw counsel on how to continuously and honestly wrestle with what it means to be patriotic as a faithful disciple of Jesus Christ in a pluralistic society. Mouw's example of humility and his common-sense wisdom is desperately needed for our time."

Luke Brad Bobo, cofounder of Pursuing the Greater Good and visiting professor at Covenant Theological Seminary

"At a time of sharp polarities and confrontational discourse, Richard Mouw's *How to Be a Patriotic Christian* could not be more timely. Drawing on his profound theological scholarship and his vibrant evangelical faith, he offers readers, in a conversational and respectful tone, a thoroughly balanced and wise discussion of how as believers we can both love our country as our home and, at the same time, be committed to the kingdom of God that embraces all nations and peoples. This is pastoral theology at its best."

Donald Senior, CP, president emeritus of Catholic Theological Union, Chicago

"As always, Richard Mouw offers his warmly humanistic thoughts on the state of America and its religiosity. This time, however, his inclusive understanding of Christian duty is especially welcome given the attraction of so many American Christians to an amoral worship of power for power's sake. A most welcome book."

Alan Wolfe, professor emeritus, Boston College, author of *The Politics of Petulance*

"Richard Mouw invites us to be Christian disciples whose faithfulness to God helps us learn how to love our nation as true patriots. Rather than encouraging idolatrous nationalism, Mouw urges us to be those who lovingly care for their nation by being willing to live well with others, see the good and bad in our past, and seek the God of the nations where the Lord has placed us. Read, agree, disagree, and put into practice what you find in these pages."

Vincent Bacote, associate professor of theology and director of the Center for Applied Christian Ethics at Wheaton College

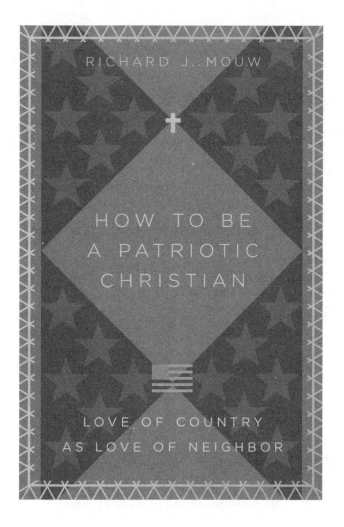

RICHARD J. MOUW

HOW TO BE A PATRIOTIC CHRISTIAN

LOVE OF COUNTRY AS LOVE OF NEIGHBOR

An imprint of InterVarsity Press
Downers Grove, Illinois

InterVarsity Press
P.O. Box 1400, Downers Grove, IL 60515-1426
ivpress.com
email@ivpress.com

InterVarsity Press® is the book-publishing division of InterVarsity Christian Fellowship/USA®, a movement of students and faculty active on campus at hundreds of universities, colleges, and schools of nursing in the United States of America, and a member movement of the International Fellowship of Evangelical Students. For information about local and regional activities, visit intervarsity.org.

Cover design and image composite: David Fassett
Interior design: Daniel van Loon
Images: 05 TGTS-Kraft-Paper: from True Grit Paper Supply
*   gold foil: © Katsumi Murouchi / Moment / Getty Images*

ISBN 978-1-5140-0402-9 (print)
ISBN 978-1-5140-0403-6 (digital)

Printed in the United States of America ∞

Library of Congress Cataloging-in-Publication Data
A catalog record for this book is available from the Library of Congress.

P	23	22	21	20	19	18	17	16	15	14	13	12	11	10	9	8	7	6	5	4	3	2	1
Y	39	38	37	36	35	34	33	32	31	30	29	28	27	26	25	24	23	22					

CONTENTS

ONE

WRESTLING TOGETHER

The title that I chose for this book announces my intention to offer counsel to Christian readers about how to be patriotic. I should make it clear at the outset, though, that this is not a how-to guide in the sense that it offers a list of steps that people should take if they want to succeed in some endeavor. I would not know how to craft such a list. The closest I can come to giving how-to advice about relating faith to patriotism is this: *keep wrestling with the questions.*

Questions like these: What does it mean to "love" our nation? If, as the Bible says, "the powers that be" are "ordained by God," does that mean we should not criticize them? What about expressions of patriotism in our church worship? And what about using religious language on events celebrating national holidays? Is "civil religion" a bad thing? What does all of this mean in times like ours, when we are experiencing deep polarizations? These topics are what I will be exploring.

My own understanding of how to be patriotic as a Christian is a work in progress. I keep wrestling with the questions, and I hope I can offer guidance to others about how to persevere in the wrestling. I know that there are people in present-day American society who see no need to do the wrestling. They can be found on both ends of the spectrum of views about patriotism. On the one end are the people who simply equate "God and country," insisting that the true destiny of the United States is to live up to our calling as "a Christian nation." On the other end are the folks who see all expression of patriotism as bad, with special disdain when love of country is connected to religious faith.

I don't know how to get the folks on those opposite ends of that spectrum to listen to each other. But I take comfort in the fact that they do represent extreme ends of a spectrum and that there is considerable room between the extremes. I find it helpful to explore the spaces between the extremes, in the confidence that the Christian message gives us resources for that kind of exploring.

The problem these days, of course, is that the public debates about patriotism are often dominated by the extremes. This has been especially true in recent years when polarization seems to have become the rule of the day. The result is that many folks—especially many of the thoughtful Christians that I know—avoid talking about these things. When I have told people that I was writing about patriotism, I have often been urged to "be careful." They worry that just by raising questions and exploring the middle spaces I will lose readers who want me to lean one way or another on the political spectrum.

I understand those concerns, but I am going to make the effort anyway. My hope is that I can use these pages as a safe place for focusing on basic Christian thoughts—drawing on biblical teachings—about what it means to be citizens in the nation where the Lord has placed us.

My use of the image of wrestling to describe what I hope we can do together here may seem a bit too combative for this kind of discussion. But given the kind of angry combat going on in these partisan days, wrestling is actually fairly tame. As a sport—and I am not thinking here about the WWE variety!—people wrestle together to test their own strength and agility. Animosity and the desire to wound the other wrestler are out of place. What I have in mind here is some spiritual and theological wrestling: testing the strength and productivity of our understandings of the obligations of citizenship. We can even set the goal that Jacob had in mind when he wrestled with the angel in Genesis 32. He engaged in the match in order to be blessed.

In working for a mutual blessing here, I need to make it clear at the outset that I am writing as a citizen of a specific nation. I am writing about being patriotic with regard to the United States of America, the nation where the Lord has placed me. My discussion here will be about American patriotism. I'm not sure I could get very far in writing about a generic sort of patriotism. I believe it is necessary to think about where we specifically are called to be patriotic. In my scholarly life I have devoted much attention in my teaching and writing to major topics and themes in political thought: theories of government, the nature of political authority, questions of religious freedom, and so on. All of that has helped me in attaining some clarity about the background—the general framework—for what I will be exploring in these pages. Good books have been written, for example, about political symbols that often have religious associations. In scholarly discussions of that sort, national flags are sometimes used as examples. I learn from those academic studies, but I find that when I start thinking about patriotism, my thoughts about flags quickly get quite personal. I reflect on how I feel and think about my country's flag, "the stars and the stripes."

ADJECTIVE AND NOUN

In choosing the two main words for my topic—*patriotic Christian*—I was very intentional in choosing *Christian* as the noun. That word identifies our fundamental identity as believers. Trusting in Christ because of what he has accomplished on our behalf is what defines us. The opening question and answer of the catechism that I learned as a child (the 1563 Heidelberg Catechism) puts it beautifully: the Christian's "only comfort in life and in death" is "that I am not my own, but belong—body and soul, in life and in death—to my faithful Savior, Jesus Christ."[1] We have by God's grace been given a new "location," being "in Christ."

Of course, the global community of people who share that common identity of being "in Christ" also live in diverse national locations. And how we understand our Christian identity in relation to those diverse contexts will differ from nation to nation.

I was made aware of these differences in a conversation that I once had with a small group of Chinese seminary students. I have visited mainland China over two dozen times, often for two weeks at a time, meeting with church and government officials, preaching in local congregations, and lecturing in the twenty-one theological seminaries of the officially approved Three-Self churches. In this particular small-group discussion the students wanted to talk about how Chinese Christians would understand how they relate to their government. One student said that as she understood the Bible's teaching, they had to "honor" the Chinese government, praying for God's blessings on the leaders. Another student strongly disagreed. He had been reading books by Dietrich Bonhoeffer, the Lutheran pastor who had been executed by the Nazis because of his Christian opposition to Hitler's evil designs. The Chinese government was not worthy of honor, he said, and true Christians must oppose the leadership, even if it means being put to death for doing so.

I was fascinated to hear their back-and-forth exchanges on this. The young woman was certainly right to cite the New Testament's mandate to honor those in authority over us. I will be discussing the importance of honoring government further on. The young man also was correct in seeing Bonhoeffer—one of my own heroes—as doing God's will in opposing Nazi ideology. I will also touch on the grounds for civil disobedience later in these pages.

What especially struck me in listening to these students talk about citizenship, though, was how real the possibility was for them of being persecuted for their convictions. They knew of actual cases of Christians being imprisoned or put under house arrest for their beliefs. Even if they were not ready to advocate for active opposition to their government, they were aware of the necessity of being very careful about what they said about the obligations of Christian citizenship. Exchanges about what it means to be patriotic for these Chinese Christian students are more urgent—and carry far more risk with them—than class discussions in Southern California.

Obviously, there are things that we need to take into account wherever we find ourselves. While the Bible tells us to honor those who are in authority over us, we also know that there come times for Christians when to obey a government is to be unfaithful to the gospel. The apostles in the early church knew this. When the authorities in Jerusalem forbade them to continue preaching the gospel, they replied: "We must obey God rather than human beings!" (Acts 5:29).

The American setting does not typically force such stark choices on us. We have the liberty to engage in serious discussions about the obligations of Christian citizenship without fearing for our safety. But there are still significant issues to pursue together, especially since we have been facing new deep divisions within the Christian community. I have Christian friends on both sides of those divides, and while I may lean one way more than the other, I confess that I do not see myself as belonging comfortably on either of the "sides." While I like to argue about the big topics, I also feel the need to get beyond the specific disagreements and find more basic principles and perspectives where Christians who take biblical authority seriously can find common ground.

I find focusing specifically on patriotism to be helpful in this regard. Even though I am acutely aware of the partisan passions, I am not convinced that our differences in dealing with political loyalties have to be as divisive as they are often thought to be. It is helpful, I think, to talk together about the proper ways to show love for our country. I also believe that we can agree as American Christians that God has indeed blessed our nation in special ways throughout our history. At the same time, I think that we can agree—that we must agree—that many of us have benefited from these blessings at the expense of others who have suffered greatly in our nation's history. This means that a legitimate love for America cannot be nurtured without also grieving and repenting for the things in our nation and its history that are unlovable.

That points to the space between the extreme ends of the spectrum. We have to keep two truths in mind: one, that it can be healthy to have a special kind of love for one's country, and two, that we have to avoid the real temptation to keep that love from taking on a kind of absolute character.

THE HIGHEST THRONE

The Bible itself tells us to avoid the extremes. And this gives us space to find ways to love our country while also engaging in some inevitable lovers' quarrels about our disagreements. It will not surprise me, though, if some readers disagree with me when I get into more detail regarding how I think we should go about loving our country. That is fine. The key is to wrestle together with important questions, even if we come up with different answers. What *is* for me nonnegotiable, though, is that we Christians must be clear that our primary allegiance, beyond what we owe the nation where we dwell as citizens, is to the kingdom of Jesus Christ. And the Bible tells us that when we come to witness the fullness of that kingdom in the heavenly regions, we will be joining our American voices with a much larger choir:

After this I looked, and there before me was a great multitude that no one could count, from every nation, tribe, people and language, standing before the throne and before the Lamb. They were wearing white robes and were holding palm branches in their hands. And they cried out in a loud voice:

"Salvation belongs to our God,
who sits on the throne,
and to the Lamb." (Revelation 7:9-10)

This is a wonderful vision of a time when we will all celebrate the fact that Jesus' throne has always been the highest seat of authority in the universe. And we will all have memories of what it was like to serve his eternal kingdom in the context of specific nations. For me, those will be American memories. So, recognizing that, I will tell some personal stories in these pages. I like an observation that the philosopher William James made in introducing his classic work *The Varieties of Religious Experience*. He informed his readers that he would be telling many individual stories from diverse spiritual autobiographies. When trying to understand religious experience, he wrote, "a large acquaintance with particulars often makes us wiser than the possession of abstract formulas."[2]

James was not against abstract formulas, and neither am I. I won't be able to avoid touching on a few of them in these pages. But I will also be offering some specific stories and examples about American patriotism, including my American patriotism. I hope that this will provide the kind of "large acquaintance with particulars" that will help to impart at least a little wisdom about what it means to love one's country in a manner that is appropriate for followers of Jesus.

Again, paying attention to individual stories is especially important right now, given the contemporary mood in our culture, with the Christian community itself divided on these matters. While I have my own perspective on these issues, I have urged my fellow Christians to set aside the stereotypes and caricatures of those with whom we disagree and to work at genuinely listening to our individual testimonies about what we see as happening in our world. For Christians it is important to find ways of listening more carefully to each other in our faith journeys. I love the line from the Christmas carol "O Little Town of Bethlehem" about "the hopes and fears of all the years" being fulfilled in the coming of the Savior.[3] Our attitude toward our country is very much a matter of hopes and fears, and I am convinced that exploring those hopes and fears in the light of biblical teaching can be a way of listening to each other more effectively.

PATRIOTIC TEARS

Some of my patriotic hopes and fears have come to the surface when I have shed tears in the presence of an American flag. One such experience happened on a visit to northern France two decades ago. My wife and I have on several occasions picked a European country in which to rent a car just to drive around for a week or so. We particularly enjoy seeing the countryside and visiting villages. This time we had decided to visit Normandy.

We had not planned to visit the site of the decisive World War II military invasion at Omaha Beach, but seeing signs pointing us in that direction, we decided to make the visit. At a certain point in our walk from the parking area we came upon the large area where over nine thousand American military men and women are buried. Many of the long rows of crosses, with a few Stars of David scattered among them, displayed both an American and a French flag at each grave. The French flags had the word *Merci* on them, expressing gratitude from local residents for the American sacrifices. Witnessing that scene, I suddenly teared up and sobbed. That response just happened, catching me off guard.

The other event occurred at an evening concert at the Hollywood Bowl, three days after the horrible events of September 11, 2001. Hollywood Bowl concerts take place under an open sky. And when the orchestra starts playing the national anthem as the program is beginning, the audience stands up, hands on hearts, looking up at the American flag on a high pole, with spotlights illuminating it. That evening, seeing the gently waving flag lit up against the darkening sky, once again I teared up and began to sob.

I have clear memories of those two occasions because they are unique experiences for me. I can't recall other times when I experienced such strong emotions of patriotism. This is not to say that I haven't had positive thoughts and feelings about being an American. For the most part I have simply taken it for granted that as a citizen I owe affection and respect for my country. At sporting events, concerts, and civic gatherings, I would always join others by standing with my hand over my heart during the Pledge of Allegiance or the singing of our national anthem, "The Star-Spangled Banner." I have seen these public rituals as the kind of things that we did as good citizens.

I do need to acknowledge in this that there are Christians who have serious theological objections to many of these rituals. I have Mennonite friends, for example, who will not join in pledging allegiance to the American flag or in singing the national anthem. There is some careful and sincere theology in their refusal to participate in such rituals, a pattern of thinking— grounded in the Anabaptist tradition of the Protestant Reformation—that takes with utmost seriousness our obligation to put our ultimate allegiance and trust in Christ and his kingdom. This perspective is also closely linked to a refusal to serve in the military out of a commitment to a nonviolent way of life.

In my career as a theological ethicist, I have considered it a special assignment to engage in dialogue with persons advocating that theological perspective. I have learned much of great importance from that engagement, and I am well aware that those dialogue partners would have objections to many things that I am setting forth in these pages. My views on patriotism draw on the theological resources of my Reformed tradition, with help also from Lutheran and Catholic resources. But I do see the dangers of going too far in participating in the existing patterns of civic engagement, and I am deeply grateful for the ways my Anabaptist friends have done their part to keep me aware of those dangers.

PROTESTING YEARS

So why did I surprise myself when I sobbed in the French cemetery and at the Hollywood Bowl? During the 1960s, when I was in my twenties, I did my share of protesting, as a graduate student on secular university campuses, in civil rights and antiwar demonstrations.

I'm not going to defend the specific views that I came to feel strongly about in those years—although basically I still hold to many of them. But I do want to support the more general case that when we come to disagree with our nation's policies or practices, it is not unpatriotic to give expression to our dissent.

My activism in those student days produced quite a bit of personal anxiety for me. This was a time when political disagreements were closely tied to intergenerational conflicts, particularly on issues relating to the Vietnam War. From many in the older generation we heard the angry rhetoric of the "America—love it or leave it!" variety. And within the evangelical community those attitudes sometimes took the form of charges that criticism of governmental policies was tantamount to a rejection of biblical teaching. As one close family member once put it to me when I said something critical about American military engagement in Vietnam: "We have to obey! Our leaders are ordained of God!"

But I was often disturbed by what I saw and heard in the protest movement as well. I was shocked on one occasion when, at an antiwar march in the nation's capital, some student activists tore down an American flag and hoisted a Vietcong flag in its place. I also found many radical slogans and chants at protest events to be disturbing.

I did feel more at home in civil rights activities. The biblical tones of Martin Luther King Jr.'s call to action were inspiring. "We shall overcome" drew on hopeful convictions about the cause of justice. Even here, though, many Christians found grounds for criticism of the civil rights cause. While Dr. King was well meaning, some of them said, he—and those of us who supported him—was simply naive about being "used by the Communists."

I look back on all of that as an important time of learning in my life, but it was difficult learning. It required struggling with lessons about faithful citizenship while also sensing the call to action.

One afternoon during my studies at the University of Chicago stands out for me in this regard. For three hours I participated in a doctoral seminar on some of the ancient Greek and Roman philosophers' understanding of civic life. They placed an emphasis on the importance of such traits as moderation, a generous spirit, and patience in our lives as citizens. When the seminar ended, I attended an outdoor student protest against a decision by the university administration to cooperate with local draft boards in ways that many of us opposed. The angry speeches at that meeting were anything but moderate, generous, and patient.

Again, I understood the passion of the protest. I do not believe that good patriots should consistently avoid anger. It is impossible to read the Old Testament prophets, or the Psalms, without seeing anger as sometimes a godly response to various forms of oppression. In my involvement in campus protests, however, I did frequently sense that the angry denunciations went beyond criticisms of specific policies to the kinds of expressions of contempt that could have the effect of harming the relationships that the Greeks and Romans argued were essential to sustaining the bonds of citizenship.

To be sure, some of those ancient philosophers also advocated courage in supporting the cause of justice in civic life. Aristotle, for one, argued that the virtue of justice could not be separated from the other virtues. I came away from that afternoon that juxtaposed scholarly reflection with political activism resolved to work at a perspective—theological as well as philosophical—that would encourage, when necessary, a loving active critique of specific governmental policies and practices. While my work during the subsequent years has often taken me into other important areas of concern, that resolve has always been present in some measure, to the point that I can say that I have been wrestling with this question throughout my career.

But patriotism is not just about our relationship to specific governmental policies and practices. It is about belonging to a community of citizens with whom we share our political allegiances—and even more important, our common humanness. Patriotism is in an important sense more about our participation in a nation than it is about loving a state. I'll give some attention to this distinction between state and nation further on.

LIKE A FAMILY

Connecting our patriotic hopes and fears to what we experience in family relations is a good place to start. The word *patriotism* is rooted in the Latin *pater*, for "father." To be patriotic is to see one's country as a fatherland. The gender issue is not important here: we can also think of our country as a motherland or, more broadly, as a homeland. All these terms denote the familial, the domestic.

With this in mind, we can note some of the aspects of our lives as members of families that are similar to aspects of our lives as citizens. A key element in patriotism is affection. We often use domestic imagery in expressing patriotic sentiments, as in the Irving Berlin lyrics, "God bless America, land that I love, . . . my home sweet home."[4]

It is helpful to pay some attention to the similarities between what we experience in our family relations and in our lives as citizens. Not only is there nothing wrong with having a special affection for one's own parents, but it is a good and natural thing. The Sinai commandment about our relationship with our parents points us to the particularity of our individual family relationships: "Honor your father and your mother" (Exodus 20:12).

Recognizing the importance of loving our own family relationships should make us aware of the Christian importance of family, but that concern should also make us mindful of practical societal and political issues, such as elder care, medical services, birthing conditions, infant nutrition, childcare, maternity leaves, adoption—and much more. These are extensions of God's simple command. We learn about the importance of families in God's plan for human beings by starting off in "my family."

There is no need here to get into specifics of a philosophy or theology of family relationships. My simple point is that we use familial language—fatherland, motherland, homeland—in speaking about our relationship to our own nation, which suggests that there are at least some illuminating parallels between belonging to a family and being the citizen of a nation.

When I was nine years old, I bought my first Mother's Day card to give to my mother. I remember going to a local store with weekly allowance money in my pocket and reading the cards to find an appropriate one. The one I chose said that my mother was "the world's greatest mother." I remember wondering if it was okay to say that to my mother since I was sure it was not literally true. I was the kind of nine-year-old Christian kid who worried a lot about God being angry with me for sins I committed, and I worried that I was telling a blatant lie in endorsing what that card said. Somewhere, I thought, there was a mother who had risked her life to rescue her child from a burning building—which would make her a greater mother than the one I had.

I decided, however, that the Lord would not be too upset with me for engaging in some exaggeration on Mother's Day. Looking back on that message to my mother, I see it as an expression of what I would now label as "hyperbolic affection." If I tell my wife, "I love you more than anything!" I am not really saying that she is more important to me than the love of Jesus.

The effusive statements that we make in talking to people whom we love also show up in expressions of patriotic sentiment. And one could argue that in principle there is nothing really wrong with that. So, maybe saying that our nation is "the greatest nation" is as harmless as my Mother's Day message to my mother.

There is a problem with the patriotic version though. My mother would not have been offended to find out that a twelve-year-old down the street told her mother that *she* was the greatest mother in the world. What was most important to my mother was how I cared about her. She did not see the mother down the street as a competitor for her own children's loyalty.

I'll put it bluntly: my mother commanded no armies. She did not use guns and bombs to defend her right to be called the best mother in the world. Nations are obviously different in this regard. They go to war with each other. And sometimes they make decisions about such matters that some citizens call into question, with the result that the questioners are accused by their fellow citizens of being unpatriotic.

Of course, in their own way families do sometimes make war on each other. Once I gave a public talk about these things, and a woman came up to me afterward to point out that I should be a little more careful about using the analogy to a family. She had suffered much in her family upbringing, she said. Among other things, she had been abused by her father, and her mother had refused to intervene. Families, as well as nations, can be dysfunctional, the woman said.

Her word of caution was important, and it points to yet another way that nations can be like families. A country doesn't just go wrong in relations with other countries. It can go wrong internally. It can be dysfunctional. Here too, then, we have to deal with whether it is always unpatriotic to criticize one's nation. It is certainly the case that genuinely loving our family members often requires that we talk to each other about where we disagree—in loving ways, it is to be hoped. To be genuinely loving in our families does not mean that there won't be deep hurts and frustrations. It just means that we are dedicated to trying to make things better rather than remaining stuck in the hurting places—or thinking that we can simply go back to what we think of as better days. The same would also seem to hold for our lives as citizens. James Baldwin put it well: "I love America more than any other country in the world and, exactly for this reason, I insist on the right to criticize her perpetually."[5]

A UNIQUE NATION?

We have to dig in a little further here. Scholars have given a lot of attention to what they refer to as *American exceptionalism.* This is the idea that the United States has a unique place among the nations of the earth. In our national culture this gets expressed by talk about our country being a "great nation" with a "special destiny."

My wife and I had a chance to think much about this issue when we encountered some anti-American sentiments while we lived for two years in Canada during my graduate school days. The negative comments about the United States came from good friends, and none of it was mean-spirited. They complained about excessive American influence on the television programs and movies that their kids watched, the impact of Washington policies on the Canadian economy, too much "American content" in classrooms and churches, and the attitudes of some visitors from the United States who were condescending about Canadian culture.

Having heard those complaints often enough, we began to see that our friends had a point. America was for them like an intimidating neighbor who was insensitive to the ways his actions affected the family next door. At the same time, however, there was affection, which was expressed in dramatic ways when President Kennedy was assassinated. Our Canadian friends not only expressed sympathy for us for our loss as American citizens, but they genuinely grieved in their own souls. They had clearly been inspired by our young president for his visionary leadership that extended beyond his own nation's borders. In short, they were ambivalent about their neighbor to the south: the real resentments were undergirded by respect for significant leadership of the United States among the nations.

I sense some of that kind of ambivalence in my own soul. I worry about some of our prideful boasts about "our great nation." But I also recognize some signs of greatness in the United States. Many of my own criticisms of my country stem from my high expectations regarding what we could accomplish with our national gifts.

"To whom much has been given, much will be required" was frequently quoted when I was growing up—my parents used it to chasten me when my report card was not up to their expectations, and schoolteachers would use it in periodic motivational talks. It was only when I grew older that I realized that it was more than a piece of popular wisdom; the thought comes from Jesus himself, in Luke 12:48 (NRSV).

The Lord's words apply to nations as well as individuals. Divine providence is surrounded in mystery, but it is possible to discern in a nation's history something of the ways in which God both blesses and tests a specific national people. God is ultimately the source of what "has been given" to a nation, and he is also the one to whom "much will be required" from the nation. There are always two questions, then, that Christians must ask in assessing a nation's degree of "greatness." How much has the nation been given? And what has it done with what it has received?

I believe that the United States has been greatly blessed among the nations. I know that some Christians worry about saying that kind of thing, but it seems obviously true to me. I am writing this while reading reports about refugees from other nations—Haiti and Afghanistan, for example—eager to be allowed to enter the United States. They rightly see our country as a place of opportunity, politically as well as materially. And they are right. It is undeniable that this is at least one of the more "blessed" nations.

But is the United States uniquely blessed? There is a history of seeing our country as a special "chosen nation." The Bible gives that title, of course, to ancient Israel. Comparing America to Israel has been common from the start, beginning with John Winthrop's much-cited sermon, preached shipboard before landing in the Massachusetts Bay, about founding a shining "City on the Hill." The Puritan settlers were sometimes depicted as having the right as God's special people to claim the "Promised Land" that was then occupied by the native "Canaanites."

We have to be clear here on one crucial point of theology. In the Bible it is the people of Israel who are seen by God as "the holy nation." The only time that phrase is used to refer to any other collective entity is in the New Testament, in the apostle Peter's first epistle. There Peter teaches that language applied in the past exclusively to the Jewish people is now extended to the Christian church, composed of both Jews and Gentiles:

> But you are a chosen people, a royal priesthood, *a holy nation*, God's special possession, that you may declare the praises of him who called you out of darkness into his wonderful light. Once you were not a people, but now you are the people of God. (1 Peter 2:9-10, emphasis added)

We must dig in a little further here. Scholars have given a lot of attention to what they refer to as American exceptionalism. This is the idea that the United States has a unique place among the nations of the earth. In our national culture this gets expressed by talk about our country being a "great nation" with a "special destiny."

The Bible takes "holy nation" status seriously, and it is significant that the only peoples who qualify for this status are Old Testament Israel and the New Testament church. No other nation qualifies. And, importantly, the New Testament sees the church as a multinational body. This is movingly expressed in the hymn to the Lamb in Revelation 5:

"You are worthy to take the scroll
    and to open its seals,
because you were slain,
    and with your blood you purchased for God
    persons from every tribe and language and people
        and nation.
You have made them to be a kingdom and priests to
        serve our God,
    and they will reign on the earth." (Revelation 5:9-10)

"You have *made* them to be a kingdom." This is about our authentic Christian identity. Yes, we are citizens of particular nations, but through the atoning work of Christ we have been given a deeper identity: citizens of a kingdom with people from other tribes and nations. When I attended church services in Canada, and when I met with theological students in China, I was bonding with "my people." Jesus made us to be citizens together in his kingdom—his "holy nation." To be sure, as I will be reminding us again and again in these pages, we also hold citizenship in different earthly nations, and God calls us to take those identities seriously. But they do not define us at the center of our redeemed natures. Belonging to the people of the Lamb is the true exceptionalism!

None of this, though, should keep us from recognizing the workings of providence in the specific history of the United States. Martin Luther King Jr. recognized this. In his powerful "Letter from Birmingham Jail," he argued that because our nation's founding vision made it clear that "the goal of America is freedom," the calls for justice in present-day life are grounded in " the sacred heritage of our nation and the eternal will of God."[6] That can't be said of many other countries although the United States is not unique in this regard. But Dr. King was right in insisting that we Americans do possess a "sacred heritage" that does bless us in special ways. To recognize this is not to engage in proud boasting about our greatness. Rather, it commits us to an active doing of God's will in our roles as citizens.

TWO

"WE THE PEOPLE"

t is impossible to imagine being a patriotic American without joining in the songs that express affection for our country. In getting ready to start writing here about patriotism, I read through the lyrics of the best known of these songs. I wanted to make sure I understood what we are being affectionate *about* when we sing these songs.

I have a reputation for quoting lines from hymns in making theological points. I pay close attention to the sentiments conveyed in hymns. Sometimes without realizing it we utter words expressing profound theological insights in our singing. At other times we express thoughts or principles in our singing that are spiritually or theologically questionable. For example, I love "What a Friend We Have in Jesus," but there is one line that bothers me: "We should never be discouraged."[1] Really? Did the person who wrote that line ever read the Psalms? Or is it good theology to say of the baby Jesus that "no crying he makes" when he lies in the manger?[2]

So for me it is a helpful exercise to pay attention to what feelings about our country we reveal when we sing American patriotic songs. In going through many of them with care recently I came up with three themes that stood out.

One theme is the love for the beauty of our natural resources: "purple mountain majesties"[3] and "rocks and rills."[4] A second is the affectionate memories of our national past: our national anthem is about seeing the American flag still waving "in the dawn's early light" over Fort McHenry after a night of bombardment during a battle in the War of 1812.[5] Our love for the "land of the pilgrim's pride"[6] is tied to the quest for religious freedom that brought many to our national shores. Third, and most important, are the national ideals that have shaped the American experience: "liberty in law," "crown thy good with brotherhood,"[7] "let freedom ring."[8]

Each of these themes deserves our affection. There is much to sing about in our national parks. There are stories about our past that inform and inspire. And the US Constitution points beyond itself to enduring ideals—"Life, Liberty, and the pursuit of Happiness"—that shape the bond that is meant to unite us as a people.

There are American political leaders whom I strongly dislike, and there are policies and laws that I personally oppose. Often what I sing in affectionate songs about the United States sets forth nicely the convictions and concerns that inform my political discontent. For example, it is because I love our fruited plains that I want to challenge some of our agricultural regulations. I get upset when stories about our national past get distorted. I want our ideals applied to all our citizens.

The three themes that characterize our patriotic songs are important to our collective sense of being a nation. The affection they express is not typically directed to political offices and policies. Those are associated with the state that governs our nation. The difference between nation and state is an important one for understanding what patriotism is about so I will now explain the difference.

PEOPLEHOOD

In a lecture that I heard him give, an African-born Christian scholar told us about growing up in a small country that had recently been released from colonial rule and was establishing itself at the time as a new independent nation. He reported that he and his fellow schoolchildren were required to memorize the opening words of the preamble to the United States Constitution, with a special emphasis on "We the people . . . in order to form a more perfect union." They were also assigned Abraham Lincoln's Gettysburg Address and then memorized these famous lines from that historic speech: "This nation, under God, shall have a new birth of freedom, and that government of the people, by the people, for the people, shall not perish from the earth."[9]

In telling us about how important these passages from American documents were for his country, he was emphasizing the importance of peoplehood as a unifying theme in the life of a nation. And he was telling us that the folks in his country were inspired by how this idea of peoplehood was so important to the forming of the United States political system. His nation was, like the United States in 1776, forming a new government. But they were doing so with a sense of being unified: "We the people" who are now forming "a more perfect union." A government that serves us best will be of, by, and for "the people." In his country during his childhood, like the United States after the American Revolution, the citizens forged an identity as a people as they worked to establish a new form of government.

Prior to the adoption of the US Constitution, the American colonies had been ruled by England. Then for a while we were held together as a loose confederation of states. Finally, recognizing the magnitude of our efforts at self-governance, "we the people" took the significant step to "form a *more perfect* union."

MANAGER AND SYMBOLIC UNIFIER

In setting ourselves free from British rule, the founders of our government made a decisive move away from the British pattern of government. That pattern is well known today for those of us who follow the adventures of British royalty. The United Kingdom has a royal family, headed by a queen or a king. There is also a Parliament, led by the prime minister, who is chosen by the political party that wields the parliamentary power. The queen or king is the leader of the *nation* while the prime minister is the head of the *state*.

We need to pay some attention to that distinction between nation and state. I have found it helpful to get at the difference in practical terms by considering an example of a person who served a role in our government and subsequently came to wish that we had something more like the British system.

George Reedy had a key role in the White House, where he served in the Lyndon B. Johnson administration, both as special assistant to the president and then as press secretary. In 1971, after he stepped away from his White House roles, he published a book in which he reflected on his experience.[10] Reedy was quite critical of the way the American presidency was structured, arguing that it has essentially the form of a monarchy.

Central to his case was his observation that the presidential office combines two roles that are typically kept distinct in other countries, particularly in parliamentary democracies. The president not only leads the state, Reedy observed, but also is the key representative of the nation. The United Kingdom is an obvious example where those two roles are strictly separate. The British queen—I have Queen Elizabeth II as my example since she has been the royal leader during my lifetime—serves as the ongoing unifier of the nation, the British people. She has no direct involvement in formulating substantive policies. Rather, her role is primarily ceremonial. To confine her influence to ceremony is not to demean her position. Ceremony, along with symbols, national days of remembrance, annual proclamations, and the like are vital to the life of a nation.

The practical processes of politics, on the other hand, are carried out in the Parliament, presided over by the prime minister. In that setting, the head of state directly engages other lawmakers. The prime minister leads the assembly on a daily basis, with his colleagues actively informing him of their opinions about policies the prime minister's party is advocating. Discussions in Parliament can be rowdy while the treatment of the royal family is typically conducted with considerable dignity.

Reedy sees the separation of powers between royalty and Parliament as representing two necessary leadership functions in a nation: the "managerial" role and that of "personifying the nation and becoming thereby the unifying factor." These two functions, he points out, are combined in the American presidency. We can see the royal-type function at play when an American president appears before a session of Congress. These are seen as ceremonial visits. The assembled legislators can applaud, but it is considered a breach of decorum to object audibly during a presidential address. Similarly, the White House has something like a palace status. It is a place where the president awards medals, hosts dinners for international dignitaries, and delivers announcements about national holidays.

Again, Reedy came to prefer the British arrangement. His day-to-day observation of the inner affairs of the White House convinced him that there was a serious problem built into the office of president. As the leader of the nation, the president is somewhat removed from the daily give and take of political negotiations—a kind of royal distancing from practical accountability for collective decision making. At the same time, the president's managerial function does give the office influence over the practical business of politics. In large part, however, this influence is exercised through officials who are non-elected members of the president's cabinet, chosen by the president. This means that those who are in direct contact with the president on policy matters are people who serve at the will of the president—yet another aspect, Reedy argues, distancing the president from the give and take of decision making.

I am not fully persuaded by Reedy's critique of the presidential office—nor by his commendation of the parliamentary system, but I do find his distinction between the two functions to be helpful for clarifying the difference between state and nation. The state has to do with practical governing: laws, policies, practices, regulations. All of that is essential to structuring the life of a large and complex community of human beings. However, I am not fully convinced by all the details of his analysis of—and proposed correctives to—the managerial aspect of the presidential job description. Most importantly, I think he attributes too much influence to the president in functioning as "the unifying factor that holds us together" as a nation. While a president does have some influence in that regard, there are many more factors that serve to reinforce a sense of being a "people." And these other factors have much to do with reinforcing a healthy sense of patriotism.

STATE AND NATION

Now here is for me a basic point: being patriotic is much more about having an affection for the nation rather than for the state. We can see this clearly in our patriotic songs. For one thing, they are most frequently sung in nonpolitical settings: athletic events, concerts, school classrooms, community organizations, Scout camps, military academies. And these songs are in turn connected to many other "peoplehood" phenomena: parades, city parks, monuments, flags, pledges, portraits of past leaders, national holidays, and civic celebrations—and more. All of this is meant to sustain an enduring experience of national identity.

Political scientists have engaged in considerable debate over the meaning of *nation* in contrast to *state*. Here are some quick thoughts about what most of them agree on. A state is a governmental system that has authority over a territory with definable boundaries. Within that territory it governs by means of a system of laws that is managed by persons in offices and roles on different levels of association (states, provinces, cities, towns). It has standards for defining citizenship and typically supports its operations by some form of taxation. It also normally manages a currency system. And it has a structure for treaties and patterns of interaction with other states.

Again, this is fairly technical, which makes the point that it is difficult to talk about what a state does in a way that evokes affectionate feelings on our part. We can certainly feel blessed by an overall pattern of government. We can love and honor our US Constitution, but we don't sing affectionate songs about, say, our national postal system or our city's zoning laws.

A nation is less easy to define, but we can say this much: a nation is a community of people who experience some kind of unity, based on shared memories of our collective past and some cultural practices and loyalties that we have in common. As citizens of a nation, we have at least a loosely defined sense of who "we" are. Sometimes, of course, the sense of collective identity is reinforced by perverse notions of what it means to be "we." But at its best a national identity is based on a common language and a commitment to the ideals of justice and civility.

This "we-ness" is expressed in some public ceremonial practices. I experienced it at Dodger Stadium, when the national anthem was played at the beginning of a baseball game. During those brief moments I glanced down the row at the other fans. We were all standing with our hands on our hearts—this was not a time when people were kneeling in protest!—and many were singing. The diversity in this particular row was striking: women, men, and children of several ages and ethnicities. All of them had a look of reverence on their faces as they directed their eyes toward the flag.

What were they revering as they paused for a patriotic moment in Dodger Stadium? Surely they did not have in mind particular governmental leaders—I think we could have gotten some passionate political arguments going in that group under different circumstances. Nor were they thinking specific thoughts about philosophies of government. Actually, I suspect they were not thinking anything. They were doing what citizens of the United States simply do in brief ceremonial moments. We engage in ritualized actions whose purpose is to reinforce a sense of unity amid considerable diversity.

In my stadium experience we did not know each other, but we were acknowledging in our actions that we had something important in common, a civic kinship. The Greek philosopher Aristotle explained that concept in ways that I find helpful. We learn our early bonding with others, he observed, in our relationships with biological kinfolk—mommy and daddy, brothers and sisters, cousins, grandparents. After a while we form friendships outside of our families: the kids we play with and our fellow students at school. We form something like a kinship relationship with them on the basis of common interests. Aristotle insisted, though, that there is a next stage. We do not really mature properly as adult human beings, he said, unless we extend those feelings of bonding to fellow citizens—people whom we may not know on an individual basis but whose shared humanity we recognize and respect.[11]

Aristotle was explaining the requirements of good citizenship in the ancient Greek city-state. But as Christians we want to insist that a truly mature awareness of that kind of kinship would extend beyond national borders, and not just to Christians. I share my God-created humanity with a village dweller in Nigeria, a victim of leprosy in Calcutta, and a shopkeeper in Barcelona. If we pay attention to what we are experiencing in our daily lives, we get special reinforcing signals of that sense of kinship in quite ordinary encounters in public places: the Muslim woman who smiles at me when she pushes her cart past me at Costco, the gay couple sitting ahead of us at the symphony concert who share our enthusiasm for the way the orchestra played a Beethoven symphony, the African American crossing guard who takes a child's outstretched hand to help her cross the street.

Casual, friendly interactions in the public square are good for reminding us of our sense of peoplehood, but they are not enough. We need to work at keeping the sense of peoplehood alive, and this requires an active "schooling" in the ways of citizenship.

CULTIVATING CIVIC KINSHIP

In my own youth this kind of schooling happened in an influential way for me by belonging to the Boy Scouts.[12] I joined the Scouts when I was about twelve, and up to that point my social world was pretty much defined by an evangelical home and congregation and daily attendance at a Christian school. For some reason—I was never sure what their motivation was—my parents encouraged me to join a Scout troop at a local Episcopal church, and my relationships expanded. I worked on merit badge projects with Latino and African American peers, and I formed a close friendship with Bobby Silverstein, the only Jewish kid in the troop. At every meeting we pledged allegiance to the flag together and heard little homilies from our scoutmaster about doing a good deed daily.

Looking back on all of that, I see the scouting movement as engaging in a program of formation for civic kinship. *Formation* has become a kind of buzzword these days. In Christian circles we talk about the importance of "spiritual formation," and ethicists have been emphasizing "moral formation" in recent years.

The Boy Scout program promoted a blend of both kinds for me, spiritual and moral, as can be seen in the twelve-point Scout Law that many of us former Scouts can still rattle off on command: "A Scout is trustworthy, loyal, helpful, friendly, courteous, kind, obedient, cheerful, thrifty, brave, clean, and reverent."[13] Not exactly the Ten Commandments or the Sermon on the Mount, but I think we Scouts all sensed that this "law" was important for our shared lives as citizens, whatever else we believed as members of different churches and temples—or of no religious affiliation at all.

That list of virtues embodies the attitudes and dispositions that can serve as a checklist for assessing the strength of the civic bond, which is reinforced by a spirit of kindness, a desire to come to the aid of persons in need, and courage in speaking out against instances of injustice.

In the evangelical world, of course, we have alternatives to the Boy Scouts these days—scouting-type movements for boys and for girls that are based on explicitly biblical convictions. I understand the benefits of groups of that sort, and, given the way that the Boy Scout and Girl Scout movements have been moving away from their founding values, I am glad that these options are available. But I have to emphasize one of the important outcomes for me in joining the Scouts: getting to know kids who were not evangelical Christians. As Christian schools and homeschooling have increased, we need to think about how the face-to-face dimensions of civic formation can be carried on. Where today are young people being formed for actually living out in a public way the virtues prescribed in the Scout Law?

Worshiping communities can do some of this. The Harvard theologian Ronald Thiemann made this point nicely when he wrote about the need for congregations to serve as "schools of public virtue" that help to form "the kind of character necessary for public life."[14] Unfortunately, though, local churches often actually fail seriously in this kind of formation since church is sometimes the place where suspicion of—even open hostility toward—folks who are not like us is encouraged.

How does the believing community work on this in our present-day context? For starters, we need to see the problem. There are new realities that make it easier for us to set up walls of separation. We are tempted to limit our social media connections to like-minded folks. We mock people engaged in alternative lifestyles. We resent new immigrant groups. An obvious way of countering all of this is to work on creating face-to-face engagement in shared projects with others—as well as finding ways to cultivate the virtues that go into, using Thiemann's phrase, "the kind of character necessary for public life."

I am deeply sympathetic to concerns of parents and grandparents who worry about their offspring being exposed to corrupting influences in our different value systems, but irreverence toward people who are created in God's image is also a corrupting influence. And in our increasingly polarized society we Christians have often been a part of the problem. When we have failed in this, it is because we have frequently espoused a strong affection for the United States without linking that to a corresponding affection for the diverse citizenry of our country. We have sometimes done this by defining ourselves as the beleaguered lovers of the "true" America—thus seeing our role as standing over against the larger society. At other times we have even engaged in crusades to take over the larger culture by promoting policies that would require others to conform—at least in their outward behaviors—to what we see as the more righteous patterns of faithful living.

This failure to acknowledge our shared peoplehood with those who are different from us can move in terrible directions. The Harvard historian Jill Lepore, who has written much about the United States as nation, has observed that in past centuries the word *nationalism* did not have the negative connotations that it has for many today but was basically synonymous with *patriotism*, and together they meant "loving the place where you live and the people you live with and wanting that place and those people to thrive." The meanings changed, however, when fascist movements emerged in Europe in the earlier part of the twentieth century. The love of nation, Lepore observes, became for many "something fierce, something violent: less a love for your own country than a hatred of other countries and their people and a hatred of people in your own country who don't belong to an ethnic, racial, or religious majority."[15]

When the love of nation takes that form, it is not only bad for our political way of life but it is bad for our standing as believers in our relationship with God. We need to find ways to demonstrate to others that we take our shared peoplehood with them seriously.

Some Christians in a Midwestern city told me about a delightfully creative way that they had found to bond with some Syrian refugee families that had recently settled in their community. They wanted to reach out to these families but did not want to come across as condescending—as "doing nice things *for* them." So they contacted some of the refugee women and asked for a favor. Some couples from their church, they said, had wanted to eat at a local Middle Eastern restaurant, but they were embarrassed to do so because they did not know how to choose items from the menu. Would some Syrian couples show them how to order, as their guests at a meal together? The refugees agreed, and this resulted in forming bonds between Christian and Muslim families, leading subsequently to interacting as guests in each other's homes. Shared dining as shared peoplehood!

THREE

HUMAN BONDS

When I was writing my book *Uncommon Decency: Christian Civility in an Uncivil World*, the word *world* in my subtitle was much on my mind. This was in the 1980s, and I was thinking a lot about how religious differences were playing a major role in the violent conflicts that loomed large on the international scene: Protestants versus Catholics in Northern Ireland, Christians versus Muslims in Eastern Europe, Israel versus Islamic nations in the Middle East. The book was published in 1992, and eight years after, it was still selling well, but attention was being given to more domestic outbreaks of incivility: road rage on California freeways, shouting matches in mall parking lots, and rudeness in the aisles of supermarkets.

In the light of that shift, several folks, including my publisher, suggested that it might be a good idea for me to update what I had written. So, at the turn of the century, I published an edition that spoke to the more recent trends.

I'm not going to do yet another revision of that book, but people do tell me now that what I wrote about the need for new measures in promoting civility was "ahead of its time." Someone even said to me recently that the mean-spirited dramas we are seeing these days in the halls of Congress, at local church congregational meetings, and on university campuses make the incivility that we were experiencing not that long ago seem tame in comparison.

CONNECTING

Of course, none of this is really new. Incivility shows up in the early pages of the Bible—with Cain's hatred of his brother Abel as an obvious case in point. Nor has it been absent in the corridors of power in the American past, with the polarization leading to the Civil War being an outstanding example. But there are new patterns that beg for new explanations, and the explanations are many. I have been a guest on talk radio shows and in podcasts and webinars where people have pointed to many factors that explain the present polarized situation. And all of them make good sense.

The internet is clearly a new formative factor. I have often written columns on contemporary events for online news sites, and when a column appears, the posted comments about my views exhibit a typical pattern. Someone will express disagreement with something I wrote, followed by someone else defending my point. However, the subsequent posts quickly turn into folks trading insults with each other, with no references anymore to what I had written in my column.

As many have pointed out, the anonymity of the internet is a key factor. There have always been gossipers, of course, but now they can say negative things anonymously and frequently—leading to particularly tragic results when the persons being bullied are vulnerable teenagers.

The social media platforms receive their fair share of criticisms for their role in fostering the present-day polarization. I see the point of the criticisms of social media while also appreciating the potential for a more positive influence.

A pastor of a small rural congregation expressed his frustration to me that people in his all-White region had no way of getting to know others of different races. "The nearest big city is seventy miles away," he said. I pointed out to him that physical miles were no longer decisive in measuring social distance. The young people in his congregation already have regular contact—through, say, TikTok, Minecraft, and Instagram—with counterparts in cities around the country, and even around the world. For example, his congregation could rather easily (with the help of tech-savvy teens!) arrange to have a shared online prayer time on a regular basis with members of a Black church in that nearest big city, praying for individual concerns in each community.

The new technologies that have come to dominate our lives have brought creative ways of connecting with other people. The challenge is whether we simply surrender to the way those contribute to increasing polarization or use them to facilitate healthier connections.

SOCIAL DECLINE

The Harvard political scientist Robert Putnam specializes in the study of voluntary associations, and he drew considerable attention to his findings in the mid-1990s in a scholarly essay with the intriguing title "Bowling Alone: America's Declining

Social Capital." He then went on to expand his case in a book, *Bowling Alone.*

Putnam used statistics about bowling to illustrate what he saw as a disturbing trend in American life. While the number of Americans who bowl has increased in recent years, he observed, participation in bowling teams and leagues has been experiencing a significant decrease. This has not been good for business at bowling alleys because, as Putnam put it, "members of leagues consume three times as much beer and pizza as solo bowlers, and the money in bowling is in the beer and pizza, not the balls and shoes."[1] More importantly, though, he pointed out that this trend means that fewer informal conversations take place than in the past in groups of people who spend time sharing the beer and pizza.

The example of participation in group bowling activities is an illustration of a more general trend. Attendance at parent-teacher association meetings has been declining, as has membership in the Rotary Club and other voluntary organizations. Specialists on the patterns of urban life have pointed out that a sense of community in neighborhoods has decreased—due, some have argued, to the disappearance of front porches and street-access driveways.

Putnam sees all of this as a depletion of what he and other commentators call "social capital," which is the fund of good will and a cooperative spirit that is nurtured by frequent face-to-face encounters with people who are not family or close friends. Putnam does acknowledge that past historical periods in American life do provide some encouragement. We have had these disruptive patterns before, he points out, followed by times of improvement. But for things to change, he argues, we have to find new ways of thinking about *we* rather than following the *I*-centered path of the widespread individualism in our culture.

DINING

I'm convinced that meals are important for building up social capital—not just times of eating but real meals *together*, dining. The decline of social meals can be seen on campuses. In the college where I was an undergraduate we ate in a dining hall, at tables where we were served our food. These days dining halls have been replaced by "campus food services" that are organized in terms of what some in the industry call "grazing stations." A typical meal consists of several visits to food-serving locations—salad, pizza, sandwiches, hot meals, a yogurt machine for a cone on the way out.

Let me say that often the food in these arrangements is excellent. I have visited many college and university campuses in recent decades as a guest speaker, and I almost always eat at least one meal in the food service facility. I must admit that the quality of food is better these days than in my own student experience decades ago, and it is pleasant to have the many "grazing" choices. But something also has been lost.

The campus mealtime pattern is often an extension of what students had experienced in their homes. Family members live busy lives. Frequently, both spouses work daily outside the home. On most evenings, sitting at a leisurely dinner together is not possible. Meals are often eaten while surfing on a smartphone or sitting in front of a TV set.

The loss here can run deep. Earlier, I mentioned Aristotle's important observation that we first learn to be bonded to others in kinship relations, with that soon expanding to friendships with people with whom we have common interests. All of that is, in turn, crucial preparation for civic kinship/friendship.

The family meal, then, is a necessary learning experience in our development as social beings. The dinner table is our first workshop in learning manners. And it gives many of us our first experiences in sitting for forty minutes with people with whom we are irritated! This is necessary developmental preparation for later getting along with fellow citizens with whom we disagree about important matters.

Maybe we can't go back to those traditional family meals of the past, the kind depicted in the old Norman Rockwell paintings. It may be, however, that the social isolation that many of us experienced during the Covid-19 pandemic actually presents us with an opportunity to find new ways of being together, including new ways of dining together: sit-down dinners on special occasions on campuses, the church potluck, breakfast Bible-study gatherings, convening in restaurants for more than a quick bite, greeting people whom we see regularly at Starbucks, one-night-a-week compulsory family meals (with no smartphones allowed!). We should do this with the awareness that finding breaks in our grazing routines is more than an exercise in nostalgia. It can be a significant way of bonding with fellow believers while also promoting a much-needed engagement with others in the public square.

MAKING LAWS

The seventeenth-century philosopher Thomas Hobbes had a very pessimistic view of our human capacity to care about the well-being of others. He stated his view boldly in his classic work *Leviathan*: "Covenants, without the Sword, are but Words, and of no strength to secure a man at all."[2] Hobbes was saying that since each human being is radically selfish, the only way to motivate us as individuals to respect the rights of others is to collectively submit to a government that will punish us if we fail to do so.

I find Hobbes's view too gloomy. For one thing, it doesn't fit my actual experience of human relationships. I see many examples in daily life of what I consider to be genuine human benevolence. Medical personnel work longer hours than are required during a pandemic, risking their own health in the process. A young couple checks daily on the elderly widower next door to see if he needs help with anything. People take time out of busy lives to volunteer at soup kitchens. Nine-year-old kids plan a birthday surprise for a schoolmate who has special needs. None of this is compelled by the threat of "the Sword."

I also believe in the reality of sin, which means that my theology encourages me to look at the deep evil we humans are capable of. Christianity requires us to look at the full range of human motivation, and individual motives are not the whole story. There are injustices that are perpetrated by the systems and collective patterns of our social existence. Here I am concentrating on how our individual loves and loyalties show up in our lives as citizens. But there is more that Christians need to be aware of in thinking about our collective social bond.

A SOCIETAL CRISIS

There are groups of our fellow citizens (including *Christian* citizens!) who have long been discriminated against in

American society. During my career, I have publicly applauded legislative efforts designed to eliminate these injustices. In recent years, though, I have also come to doubt the ability of legislative measures by themselves to bring about permanent change. Laws can be inconsistently applied, and they can even be revised or revoked. Or, perhaps worse, they can be kept on the books while being ignored by those in charge of administering the laws.

It takes vigilance to ensure that the true goals of our legal measures are pursued. Effective legislation must be undergirded by a shared commitment to the flourishing of our life together. The classic understanding of a just society is one which grants "to every man his due."[3] And the due of all citizens is to be treated with dignity as human beings who—as our Declaration of Independence put it—"are endowed by their Creator with certain unalienable Rights, [and] that among these are Life, Liberty and the pursuit of Happiness."

For a society to flourish, its citizens need to *want* justice, to nurture a commitment to honoring our fellow human beings. The maintenance of a healthy social bond takes moral and spiritual work. And it seems obvious to many who monitor closely the patterns of our collective interactions that we Americans have not been doing the necessary work.

This work also requires personal encounters. Some friends of mine, given to quite conservative political convictions, told me what happened when they mentioned their concerns about the Black Lives Matter movement to a Black Christian friend of theirs. He held many of the same political and theological views that they did so they felt safe in airing their complaints to him. He told them he agreed with many of their criticisms but that he would like to sit with them for an evening when he and his wife could share with these friends some of their experiences in race relations. They scheduled the evening, and my friends reported to me that it had been a transforming experience when their fellow Christians related their painful episodes of prejudice and discrimination.

Encounters of this sort are not only nice things to do. They are necessary for getting a better sense of reality. The evening those couples spent together, as painful as it was for each, was necessary for all of them, for those who heard the stories as well as for those who told them.

Another practical example: I was once approached by members of a congregation in an American town near the border with Mexico, asking whether I could spend a weekend sharing my thoughts about issues relating to "undocumented residents" living in their community. Some members were eager to advocate with local officials on behalf of the immigrants while others were strongly opposed. When I met with the congregants, it became clear that they were divided over political allegiances. In our concluding session I told them that while I could not resolve their ideological differences, there was one thing that they could do without either group's compromising its political convictions. They could get to know some of these local residents, simply to see if there were ways that as Christians they could minister to their real human needs.

Months later the members of the congregation contacted me to tell me what had happened. They—people of both "sides"—met a young couple who would soon be having their first child. At one point the young husband tearfully confessed that he was deeply fearful of what might happen when his wife went into labor. He was afraid that he would be stopped by the police while rushing her to a hospital and that the law officers would then deport him because he did not have legal documentation.

The congregation made a commitment to the couple. They gave them several of their phone numbers and urged the husband to let them know when she had to be driven to the hospital—any time of day or night. He did call when the time arrived, and members of the congregation, who had been praying faithfully for the couple, drove them to the hospital and kept the others informed about the birth. As a result, they bonded with the couple's newborn daughter in multiple ways, treating the child as "one of their own." Eventually it was decided all around that their prayers had to take the form of advocating on behalf of the young couple with local officials.

In describing contemporary American culture, social commentators these days frequently use words like *tribalism, polarization,* and *culture wars.* It is a good question, of course, whether things are worse today than they have been in the past. But, as already noted, the growth of social media has certainly provided new opportunities for airing our grievances and hostilities. The social bond has always been fragile, but these days it appears to many that the bond is deteriorating to the point of creating deep and permanent fractures.

I am greatly concerned about the mean-spiritedness that characterizes so much of our present-day national life, but I am not prepared to concede that the situation is beyond repair. I recognize that the problem goes deep. Actually, I see it as going deeper than many of the social critics acknowledge.

But it is precisely the deep nature of our crisis that gives me hope. The answer is not simply to elect different candidates to our public offices. Nor will new rules and regulations about "hate speech" and "internet ethics" bring adequate solutions. Those can be worthy strategies, but they do not get to the depth of the crisis. There is a spiritual dimension that must be addressed, and positive steps can be taken by people of faith who have access to the spiritual resources that can help us. As believers, we can take much hope from biblical reminders of how God has often acted in surprising ways in seemingly impossible situations: "Where sin increased, grace increased all the more" (Romans 5:20).

THE REACHES OF LOVE

Earlier I mentioned the importance of undergirding our patriotic commitments with a sense of civic kinship. I am very fond of that concept. That notion of kinship can take us a long way in understanding our bonds to other human beings. We have strong family ties to other Christians, wherever they are. But we also have deep bonds with *all* human beings—persons who, whether they acknowledge it or not, are created in the image and likeness of the God and Father of Jesus Christ. Attending a baseball game at Dodger Stadium, visiting a tourist site in India, shopping for groceries—these too are, in the broader human sense, family visits.

But we need more than a formal acknowledgment of kinship. The Bible pushes further by asking us actively to love our neighbors—which, as we will see, includes all human beings. The challenge, of course, is that talk about extending love that far can come across as mere sentimentality. Do we really want to propose to members of Congress that Democrats should love Republicans? Won't we make fools of ourselves if we show up at city council budget hearings to plead for a loving allocation of public funds? What does love have to do with what goes on in traffic court on a given day? And even more: When I watch a National Geographic feature about residents of a rainforest in what is for me a remote part of the world, do I really have to find ways to love the folks I am seeing on the screen? Does *love* have any realistic operational meaning in those contexts?

But Christians cannot give up on an expansive understanding of love. The Bible is serious on this subject: love applies to our collective lives as well as to our personal relations. While the Great Commandment is that we love God with all of our being, the second commandment, as Jesus reminds us, "is like it": "'Love your neighbor as yourself'" (Matthew 22:39). And we have a lot of neighbors whose names and faces are completely unfamiliar to us.

Again, the idea of love seems to apply easily to personal relationships. Love for a spouse, child, parent, friend, or even the person who lives two doors away from us—each of these is a matter of personal affection toward a specific person. But there are other kinds of loves. I have talked about America as the "land that I love,"[4] even though I can't spell out the meaning of my patriotic love in terms of specific affections. I know a football coach at a Christian university who encourages his players to "love" the opposing team each weekend. For several days before the game the team members pray that it will be a well-played competition on both sides, and that there will be no mean-spirited actions on the field.

When Jesus was asked to explain what it means to love one's neighbor, he told the parable of the Good Samaritan. It's clear in this story that the Samaritan's commendable love of his neighbor was not a subjective affection for a person he knew. Unlike the priest and the Levite in Jesus' story—the folks who had simply passed by without showing concern for the wounded man—the Samaritan stopped to attend to the person's wounds and even arranged for further health care. The whole point of the story is that he did this even though the more intimate bonds of personal friendship, or shared ethnicity or citizenship, were not present.

My favorite theologian, the sixteenth-century Reformer John Calvin, captured the expansive character of this kind of love nicely. Calvin observed that as sinners we are "all too much inclined to self-love," and in our Christian lives we need to work hard at treating our neighbor in a loving manner. Our "neighbor," Calvin says, "includes even the most remote person," extending beyond "the ties of kinship, or acquaintanceship, or of neighborhood." It is a love that should "embrace the whole human race without exception in a single feeling of love," with "no distinction between barbarian and Greek, worthy and unworthy, friend and enemy, since all should be contemplated in God, not in themselves."[5]

That last comment about seeing our neighbors as they are "contemplated in God" is important to highlight. God sees every human being as his creation—fashioned in his image and likeness. That means that God wants us to go beyond the surface differences among our fellow human creatures to see the underlying humanity that we share with them.

But God does not just see a generic humanity—he sees persons in their unique individuality. There is a delightful story that I once heard someone tell about Pope John XXIII when he was still Cardinal Roncini, the leader of the Catholic community in Venice. On a typical evening a young priest would meet with the cardinal as he was enjoying some after-dinner wine to report on things that had happened that day in the local parishes. On this particular evening the young assistant was agitated as he told the future pope about the actions of a rebel priest who was saying negative things about the cardinal. As the priest reported this, the future pope just calmly sipped his wine.

Finally, the assistant paused and then addressed the cardinal in a loud voice: "Doesn't this bother you, your Eminence? This priest is trying to undermine your authority!" The cardinal took the last sip of his wine and held up the crystal goblet. "Whose glass is this, Father?" The young priest replied, still with an agitated tone: "It's yours, your Eminence!" The cardinal then tossed the goblet on the floor, and it shattered into many pieces. "And now whose goblet is it?" he asked. "It's still yours," the young man responded. Then the future pope spoke in a quiet voice: "That priest you have been talking about was created by the Lord. Presently, he is quite broken, but he is still a child of God."

Each human being is a special creation of the Divine Artist. And artists have an affection for what they have created, even when the work of art has been subsequently damaged. As Jesus taught us, the Lord knows every sparrow who falls to the ground, and, the Savior observed, if that is the case, how much more does the heavenly Father know and care about each unique human being (Matthew 10:29-31)?

I admit that as soon as I make that point, questions crowd my mind. But what about Hitler? And the Queen Jezebels of our present world? And the folks who enjoy living off the profits they make in running sex-trafficking businesses? Does God love each of them in their brokenness? Important questions.

Romans 1:18 and following make it clear that God does give some people over to the wicked forces that have come to control their lives. We can't simply overlook acts of vicious racism or the willful act of a rapist. There is a lot to explore on this subject, but this much seems clear to me: while there are real cases where we must oppose serious misdeeds that people perform, doing our best to put an end to their evil designs, we often get to that point too quickly. I have made a similar point on the subject of civility. People ask me, "But aren't there limits to the need for civility? Aren't there situations where people have become so abusive that being civil toward them is inappropriate?" And the answer is, of course there are. But my clear sense is that more often than not we err on the side of giving up too quickly on civility. Similarly, we—and especially we Christian people—cannot be accused of typically having shown too much love toward folks with whom we differ on important concerns.

WAYS TO CONTEMPLATE

In the comment I quoted from John Calvin, he points us in a helpful direction when he says that our fellow human beings "should be contemplated in God, not in themselves." The call to *contemplation* is an important one. Contemplating takes effort. It requires focus, attending, using our imaginations.

I admire Christians who do the hard work of cultivating practices of contemplation.

Here, for example, is testimony by the late Henri Nouwen, whose writings have helped so many of us in our personal spiritual journeys. In a collection of meditations that he wrote while on an extended spiritual retreat, Father Nouwen tells us what he experienced during many hours devoted to prayer:

> Prayer is the only real way to clean my heart and to create new space. I am discovering how important that inner space is. When it is there it seems that I can receive many concerns of others. . . . I can pray for many others and feel a very intimate relationship with them. There even seems to be room for the thousands of suffering people in prisons and in the deserts of North Africa. Sometimes I feel as if my heart expands from my parents traveling in Indonesia to my friends in Los Angeles and from the Chilean prisons to the parishes in Brooklyn.
>
> Now I know that it is not I who pray but the Spirit of God who prays in me. . . . He himself prays in me and touches the whole world with his love right here and now. At those moments all questions about "the social relevance of prayer, etc." seem dull and very unintelligent.[6]

I have frequently used that quotation from Nouwen in my writings and speeches, pointing to the way in which it illustrates the power of prayer for expanding our consciousness of human realities. I have to confess, though, that I am not very good at the kind of prayer life that Nouwen describes. Truth be told, I find the paragraph I just quoted to be spiritually intimidating. In his praying he cultivates feelings of holy intimacy with prison populations, nomadic peoples in African deserts, and Brooklyn congregations. I don't know how even to get started in creating that kind of spiritual space in my heart and mind.

To say that is not to question the sincerity of Nouwen's testimony, but it is to acknowledge that he is one of a select group of spiritually gifted people who inspire awe in me as I observe them from a distance. Admiring Nouwen is for me much like watching a football game on TV and seeing a tight end on a full run reach out to catch the ball with his fingertips while being crowded by defensive players from the other team—then crossing the goal line while still hugging the ball closely to his chest. That kind of performance fills me with wonder.

That kind of wonder can serve as something more than entertainment, however, if it motivates me to make at least a small positive move in a healthier direction—a little more time on the exercise bike the next day, for example. The example set by Nouwen can do a similar thing for me, by inspiring an increase in my spiritual exercise. My move may be a fairly modest one, but it should at least sharpen my sense of focus and expand my capacity for prayerful imagination.

Having had the privilege of international travel, I have been able to make room in my heart for individuals in other countries, but there are many regions of the world where I know nothing about the citizens or their daily lives. It's not that I shut these other folks out—it is a matter of focusing on those who have captured my attention because of experiences that have come my way. Each of us should have a focus on at least some people who are different from ourselves but with whom we share a common humanity. And we need to create the experiences that make the focus happen.

A friend told me about a predominantly White Midwestern congregation where the members had gotten caught up in some passionate arguments about whether Black citizens are victims of "systemic racism." Around that time a family who had been traveling in the Southwest came back with glowing reports of a Native American congregation they had visited—a church that the Midwestern congregation had been supporting through their denominational mission budget. Prayer requests from the Native Christians began to be shared with the folks in the Midwest, and soon the White members were praying regularly for concerns on the reservation that were similar to those that had been debated in the "systemic" arguments.

That development was not a full solution regarding topics dealing with the plight of racial minorities in the United States. But the good thing was that the congregation had discovered a shared focus for taking some of those issues seriously in prayers for people whom they could mention by name—and resulting in actions that were inspired by those prayers.

Not all of us, of course, can spend significant time in other nations or take advantage of reports from friends who have visited a reservation in the Southwest. But we can decide to read novels by Black authors or visit websites that keep us informed about the plight of Muslims in Myanmar or monitor and support an orphanage in Sierra Leone. These strategies can assist us in personalizing the realities faced by a community of fellow human beings who are different from ourselves.

On the subject of race relations, my own focus began as a seven-year-old baseball fan. Raised in a part of New Jersey close to New York City, I became a fan of the Brooklyn Dodgers early on. When I was seven years old, Jackie Robinson joined the team as the first Black player in the major leagues, and I immediately began cheering him on.

Having formed that enthusiasm for him, I was deeply shocked and puzzled when, at a family gathering, some of my relatives, several of them also Dodger fans, expressed their disapproval that the Dodgers would add "one of them" to the team. "Those folks have their own teams and their own league—why do they have to play in ours?" was one comment that especially disturbed me. I was too young to articulate a coherent perspective on the matter so I remained silent, but I sensed that there was something deeply wrong with what I was hearing. I recall praying in my bedroom that evening that God would bless Jackie Robinson and forgive my relatives for what they had said. Not long after that I felt that at least the first half of that prayer was answered when Jackie stole home during a game with the Pittsburgh Pirates!

My interest in Jackie Robinson went a little bit beyond following his career on the diamond. I bought a ten-cent comic book about his life and learned about his growing up—a "shoeshine boy" who got closer to baseball by getting a job selling hot dogs at the stadium—and about his marriage to Rachel and the three children they parented.

I hadn't tied all of that in with spirituality at the time, but many years later I learned something about the need to pray for the families of professional athletes from the Black evangelist Tom Skinner. Tom had served as a chaplain for one of the professional football teams, and he described for me the personal challenges of athletes who were "sold"—a painful verb for many Black players—by one team to another. The news of the sale sometimes came as a surprise to the athlete himself, and frequently the change occurred while his children were in school, so his family had to face being suddenly up-rooted from their social networks. Tom spoke passionately about the need for praying for the families of the athletes for whom we cheer. I now see this as a focused way for sports fans to make room in their spiritual lives for the genuine human concerns of others.

My childhood fascination with Jackie Robinson did not amount to civil rights activism—although I did get repri-manded around that time by a security guard when on a family trip to Florida I deliberately drank from a water fountain marked "Colored." I had at least made some room in my heart for persons who experienced racial discrimination.

Christians need to find practical ways for making room in our lives for the concerns of people whose life situations are different from our own. Even praying for our favorite athletes can give us the kind of focus that enables us to see our neighbors as they are "contemplated in God"!

FOUR

WHERE "HONOR IS DUE"

I f someone were to conduct a survey to see which biblical passage gets cited most often when American Christians talk about their relationship to their government, I have no doubt what the winner would be: "Give back to Caesar what is Caesar's and to God what is God's" (Mark 12:17).

This should not be surprising. It is the one thing we can quote from Jesus himself in addressing the political situation of his day. And although it is about a specific political authority—he was asked about Caesar, and he responded by naming Caesar—it does have the feel of a general principle. Give to your government what it rightly has coming to it, and give to God what rightly belongs to God.

While I have no problem accepting that principle as stated, affirming it does leave us with questions about how to apply it. And when we look at the New Testament context in which Jesus set forth that principle, it is clear that he meant for us to ask questions about what he intended. This "give back to Caesar" comment by Jesus is recorded in three different Gospel accounts: Matthew 22:21, Mark 12:17, and Luke 20:25.

Each time it is made clear that Jesus gives this directive when his opponents are trying to trip him up. They are asking him questions that will get him into trouble with some group, no matter what he answers. In Luke's account, for example, the Caesar question is the second of three that are asked of Jesus, all recorded in the same chapter. The first question is about his own authority: Does it come from God or is it of human origin (Luke 20:2)? It is meant as a trick question. If he says it comes from God, he can be charged with blasphemy, but if he says it is of purely human origin, he will be undercutting his ministry. Jesus avoids the dilemma by coming back with his own question to them. He asks them about the baptism of John the Baptist: Was it authorized by heaven or by human beings (Luke 20:4)? They knew that Jesus had turned the tables on them with his own trick question.

> They discussed it among themselves and said, "If we say, 'From heaven,' he will ask, 'Why didn't you believe him?' But if we say, 'Of human origin,' all the people will stone us, because they are persuaded that John was a prophet."
>
> So they answered, "We don't know where it was from."
>
> Jesus said, "Neither will I tell you by what authority I am doing these things." (Luke 20:5-8)

In the third confrontation the Sadducees posed a question to Jesus about a woman who had been married seven times, to seven brothers. When the dead are eventually raised to life, they asked, who will be her husband? Jesus responded that in the age of the resurrection, people will "neither marry nor be given in marriage" (Luke 20:35). His opponents did not know what he meant—nor have the scholars since then who have debated the topic. Will the earthly relationships between wives and husbands be eradicated in the afterlife? Does it mean no new marriages? Will the formal marriage relationship continue but without sexual intimacy? All these options have been proposed at one time or another in Christian history, with no real consensus about what Jesus meant—which is clearly what Jesus intended in this exchange with the Sadducees.

The injunction to "give back to Caesar" must be understood in its context, as the story has its place between these two other confrontations. Here too, as all three Gospel accounts make clear, Jesus' opponents are trying to trap him into saying something that will get him in trouble. In this case, though, the trap is a dangerously political one: in asking him whether it was legitimate for the Jewish people to pay taxes to the occupying Roman government, their intention was, the Bible says, "to catch Jesus in something he said, so that they might hand him over to the power and authority of the governor" (Luke 20:20). If Jesus said that it was not legitimate to pay taxes to Caesar, he would be in trouble with the Romans. If, on the other hand, Jesus said he approved of paying the taxes, he would be offending many of his people, who resented the Roman occupation.

Jesus' answer left them puzzled, for he left open what rightfully *does* belong to Caesar. Does Caesar putting his official seal on something mean that it now rightly belongs to him? Obviously not—any more than the United States issuing currency means that we should not put dollar bills in the offering plate that is passed in a church service. What is required for Christians, then, is to think carefully about how to live our lives as citizens in God-honoring ways.

THE POWERS THAT BE

Romans 13 is also often quoted by Christians when talking about the role of government, and, like the "give back to Caesar" passage, it is typically used to encourage believers to refrain from dissenting from the dictates of government. Here are the first two verses, using the well-known language of the King James Version:

> Let every soul be subject unto the higher powers. For there is no power but of God: the powers that be are ordained of God.
>
> Whosoever therefore resisteth the power, resisteth the ordinance of God: and they that resist shall receive to themselves damnation." (Romans 13:1-2 KJV)

Does this mean that we must conform to whatever our government requires of us because God has "ordained" the authorities to exercise power over us? No, that is not the message. Indeed, when we think of Christians striving to be faithful to God's will under difficult political conditions, most of us would insist on the need to say much more. I certainly would not have counseled Dietrich Bonhoeffer in Nazi Germany, or Black South African believers during the apartheid era, simply to "be subject unto the higher powers" since God has ordained those powers to work for their good.

Truth be told, a careful reading of the Romans passage shows that Paul is telling us about what God expects the political powers to be doing if they are actually faithful to the purposes for which he "ordains" them. Here is the rest of the passage, with the significant phrases highlighted: "For rulers hold no terror for those who *do right*, but for those who do wrong. Do you want to be free from fear of the one in authority? *Then do what is right* and you will be commended. For the one in authority is *God's servant for your good*" (Romans 13:3-4).

The problem, of course, is that this description is not true of all governments. Too often political authority is not exercised by those who are "God's servant for your good." They do just the opposite of what is being described by the apostle, by rewarding those who do evil and punishing those who do good. The Bible and church history are full of examples of persons who resisted political authorities who were not functioning in the way that the apostle describes. In the Old Testament Daniel disobeyed a corrupt government, as did the young men who were sent to the fiery furnace. In the New Testament the apostles were willing to go to prison when they were commanded by authorities not to preach, and later thousands of martyrs faced ridicule, hungry lions, the stake, and the sword rather than submit to idolatry, defilement of worship, or the dishonoring of the name of their Lord.

Another important element of this Romans 13 passage has to do with the counsel for believers to actively "do right," which has a meaning that is independent of mere obedience to governmental dictates. It is not up to governmental leaders to decide what counts as doing "right"—we know that by consulting the will of God.

This means actively doing that which is good in the Lord's sight. The active dimension is important for Christian patriotism. Truly showing love for the United States of America is not simply learning to "live and let live" while periodically doing one's duty by paying taxes and remembering to vote. Loving one's country must take the form of actively engaging in doing "right." In this context the apostle is emphasizing the witnessing aspect of doing the right sorts of things. We are called to show others in our society that we care about the well-being of the larger community. This showing requires our finding creative ways of cooperating with others to demonstrate our commitment to the common good.

EXILED LIVING

This active dimension of patriotism is highlighted in another New Testament passage, and this passage offers what I see as the most detailed discussion in the Bible of the duties of citizenship: the counsel of the apostle Peter in the second chapter of his first epistle. Since I will be commenting on this passage verse by verse, I will start by quoting it here in its entirety:

> Dear friends, I urge you, as foreigners and exiles, to abstain from sinful desires, which wage war against your soul. Live such good lives among the pagans that, though they accuse you of doing wrong, they may see your good deeds and glorify God on the day he visits us.
>
> Submit yourselves for the Lord's sake to every human authority: whether to the emperor, as the supreme authority, or to governors, who are sent by him to punish those who do wrong and to commend those who do right. For it is God's will that by doing good you should silence the ignorant talk of foolish people. Live as free people, but do not use your freedom as a cover-up for evil; live as God's slaves. Show proper respect to everyone, love the family of believers, fear God, honor the emperor. (1 Peter 2:11-17)

Peter emphasizes here some of the same things that we saw in Paul's instructions in Romans 13. He repeats the stress on active doing. Christian citizenship, he says, requires the performing of "good deeds" in public life. He also affirms the teaching that an essential function of a government is "to punish those who do wrong and to commend those who do right."

But Peter adds some important elements that are not made explicit elsewhere in the New Testament. For one thing, he addresses us as "foreigners and exiles." In doing so he is alluding to the time in the Old Testament when the people of Israel were taken captive to live in the pagan city of Babylon, and the apostle is repeating the kind of advice that the Lord gave to those Babylonian "foreigners and exiles." So we will take a brief look at how God wanted his people to handle the exile in Babylon.

Being forced to relocate from Jerusalem to the pagan city of Babylon was deeply traumatic for the ancient Israelites. In this new urban setting they had no temple for their worship of the true God, and the laws and practices of the city were strange to them. The Jewish people found it difficult to grasp how they could maintain obedience to the Lord in their daily lives, as is clear in this psalm of lament that was written during this period:

By the rivers of Babylon we sat and wept
    when we remembered Zion.
There on the poplars
    we hung our harps,
for there our captors asked us for songs,
    our tormentors demanded songs of joy;
      they said, "Sing us one of the songs of Zion!"

How could we sing the songs of the LORD
  while in a foreign land? (Psalm 137:1-4)

Their cry for help was genuine, and God did not leave them without an answer to their poignant plea. The Lord used the prophet Jeremiah to give them instructions about how they could sustain their identity as God's chosen people in this new setting. The Lord wanted them, the prophet said, to build residences, to plant gardens, and to marry off their sons and daughters, so that they could "increase in number there; do not decrease" (Jeremiah 29:5-6).

Then Jeremiah adds this significant mandate from the Lord: "Also, seek the peace and prosperity of the city to which I have carried you into exile. Pray to the LORD for it, because if it prospers, you too will prosper" (Jeremiah 29:7).

Significantly, the Hebrew word translated here as "peace and prosperity" is *shalom*, a word with rich meaning. It contains ideas of justice, peace, general well-being. It is not only about individual happiness but also about a collective human flourishing. And this flourishing is not simply something that the Israelites were to wish for. They were to seek it—God was calling them to actively promote shalom, accompanied by prayers on behalf of their fellow citizens.

That the apostle Peter was giving a similar instruction to the New Testament community of "foreigners and exiles" is seen in the four direct commands he gives to his readers: "Show proper respect to everyone, love the family of believers, fear God, honor the emperor" (1 Peter 2:17). Two of these commands are central to Christian identity: a holy fear of the Lord and an intimate sacrificial love for the family of believers.

But the other two range more broadly, with the same content and scope of Jeremiah's call for actively promoting the shalom of the larger society. Indeed, Peter uses the same Greek verb, *timaō*, which means "have regard for the well-being of," to stipulate the "honor" we owe our government as well as the "proper respect" we owe all our fellow citizens. We honor our political authorities because God has given them the authority to act for our good. The call to honor these authorities means that we should want them to flourish in performing their duties. They may not know that the authority that they exercise comes from the Lord, but when they promote the policies and practices that create conditions for societal health, while also discouraging doing what is bad for human community, they are not just serving their citizenry. They are serving themselves by performing the functions for which God has designed political leadership.

In Romans 13 Paul says to "give to everyone what you owe them" (Romans 13:7), and here Peter expands on that to tell us that in our honoring of political authorities we are acknowledging the purposes for which the Lord has ordained them to serve. The emperor is deserving of our honor when the emperor is also engaged in honoring all who have been placed under his care. We owe honor, not only to the political powers but to all our fellow citizens. The political powers are worthy of honor when they honor those of our fellow human beings whom God also calls *us* to honor.

TEARS IN PYONGYANG

In August 2011 I visited North Korea. The short version of the story is that I accompanied a Korean American business leader, a devout Christian, who learned that two villages in the northernmost part of North Korea had recently been devastated by landslides and floods, and that little children were dying of starvation every day. Through a contact in the North Korean government, he arranged for several tons of food to be shipped to those villages, with the understanding that he would be allowed to visit those villages to confirm that the food had been made available to the folks living there. The government agreed, and he invited me to accompany him.

We were driven by a government official to the villages, a ten-hour journey each way. Then we spent the weekend in Pyongyang, the North Korean capital, before returning home. On Sunday our government "minders" arranged for us to attend a Christian worship service in a church that had been built by missionaries in the early years of the twentieth century. We were told that this church was one of four legally permitted places of worship in the country. At the service we met Canadian and German diplomats who confirmed that they attended that service each week.

When we walked into the sanctuary, the robed North Korean choir was singing (in Korean) "Jesus Paid It All."[1] Midway through the service they sang "What a Friend We Have in Jesus."[2] When they were singing the verse with the words "in His arms He'll take and shield thee, thou wilt find a solace there," I noticed that a young woman in the front row of the choir had cheeks wet with tears as she sang about her relationship with Jesus.

Suddenly it occurred to me that thus far I had been seeing my presence in that church service as that of a tourist who was observing how people in a totalitarian nation engaged in religious worship. But now in the tears on the cheeks of that choir member I saw something different. I was looking at a sister in Jesus Christ. This was not a tourist experience—it was for me a family gathering. The woman with the tears was one of my people.

I often pray for that young woman whom I saw weeping. Peter tells me that I must love her so I ask the Lord regularly to hold her close in his arms and to shield her. And to keep her strong in the faith. I am not a fan of the North Korean government. It is a wicked regime. But that image is a reminder to me that I have family in North Korea. In that church service I had a new experience of what it means to love the family of believers as I sensed my Christian kinship with this worshiping community. All of this led me to think in some new ways about the apostle's mandate for Christians to honor political authorities while also honoring all human beings who are subject to those authorities.

When we had visited two villages in the northern part of the country, we were greeted by the villagers, mostly women and children. It was clear that they were deeply grateful for the food that my friend had provided. In visiting their villages to confirm that they had actually received the supplies, we were honoring them.

But what about honoring their government? I don't think of the North Korean government as worthy of honor. It is engaged in doing much evil, regularly rewarding those who do evil and punishing those who do good.

I do wish, however, that I could talk to my Christian sister in the choir about this. I'm sure she knows how her political leaders treat so many of her fellow believers, sometimes putting a citizen to death simply because the person possesses a Bible. It would not surprise me if she told me that she prays earnestly that her government would turn from its wicked ways to honor those who worship the true God. I would hope, however, that she also prays for her non-Christian fellow citizens, like the families in those two villages we had visited.

The very fact that at least some Christians are allowed to gather for worship in Pyongyang, though, is reason also to offer a measure of honor to the authorities who permit it. In one local context, under the authority of a viciously atheistic government, people are publicly praying, singing about Jesus, and reading the Scriptures. We can pray that at least this small gesture of rewarding those who do good will not be reversed.

North Korea and the United States represent very different —even clashing—modes of government. In each case Christians must wrestle with how biblical teachings regarding the believing community's relationship to governing authorities apply—and think about what it might mean in each case for us to love the specific countries where God has placed us.

FIVE

THE SCOPE OF GOVERNMENT

The biblical passages we have been looking at emphasize our obligation to honor those governments that are doing what God has "ordained" them to do. A key governmental duty, we have seen, is to encourage good behaviors and discourage the bad. But we have to think about what this means regarding the proper limits of government. We certainly should not expect—or even want—governments to reward *all* good deeds and punish *all* evil ones. That is much too broad an assignment. A seventh-grade student plans a surprise birthday celebration for a disabled fellow student who has often been bullied. Certainly a good deed—even an honorable one. But we should not expect a reward for her from the local government. A shopper at a grocery store may say something rude to the checkout person. That is a bad thing—but it is not the sort of thing that should motivate us to dial 911 to call for the police.

There are boundaries for defining proper governmental activity. And Christians should reflect on the boundaries that determine those categories in the light of God's purposes for establishing political authority. In doing that, furthermore, we can achieve a better understanding of the divinely desig-nated purposes of government in our lives because the Bible does allow for more governmental responsibility than simply rewarding and punishing behaviors.

The Bible speaks to those broader purposes. Psalm 72 is one of the places where several of those purposes are listed as the psalmist prays that a king will exercise his authority in ways that are pleasing to God:

> Endow the king with your justice, O God,
>   the royal son with your righteousness.
> May he judge your people in righteousness,
>   your afflicted ones with justice.
> May the mountains bring prosperity to the people,
>   the hills the fruit of righteousness.
> May he defend the afflicted among the people
>   and save the children of the needy;
>   may he crush the oppressor.
> May he endure as long as the sun,
>   as long as the moon, through all generations.
> May he be like rain falling on a mown field,
>   like showers watering the earth.
> In his days may the righteous flourish
>   and prosperity abound till the moon is no more.
>   (Psalm 72:1-7)

Admittedly, Psalm 72 contains some flowery language—it certainly would be a bit much for a prayer at a city council meeting! This was likely meant originally as a poetic cele-bration of Solomon's kingly rule—and as Christian believers we can also see themes here that point us to the coming of Christ, who will indeed reign "as long as the moon."

It is interesting to look at some similarities between this psalm and the purposes of government cited in the first sentence of the preamble to the United States Constitution:

> We the People of the United States, in Order to form a more perfect Union, establish Justice, insure domestic Tranquility, provide for the common defense, promote the general Welfare, and secure the Blessings of Liberty to ourselves and our Posterity, do ordain and establish this Constitution for the United States of America.

This is a summary statement of the tasks of government that the Constitution goes on to delineate. The four general tasks that the preamble gives in its brief overview have some parallels with the prayer of Psalm 72. See in figure 1 the parallels I have in mind.

THE PREAMBLE	PSALM 72
We the People of the United States . . . establish Justice,	Endow the king with your justice, O God . . . May he judge your people in righteousness, and your afflicted ones with justice.
insure domestic Tranquility,	May the mountains bring prosperity for the people, the hills the fruit of righteousness.
provide for the common defense,	May he defend the afflicted among the people, and save the children of the needy; may he crush the oppressor.
promote the general Welfare, and secure the Blessings of Liberty to ourselves and our Posterity	May he be like rain falling on a mown field, like showers watering the earth. In his days may the righteous flourish and prosperity abound till the moon is no more.

Figure 1. Parallels between the preamble and Psalm 72

First, the psalmist prays that God might endow human governments with justice, just as the writers of the preamble wish to "establish Justice" in their new country. Political leadership is responsible for sustaining a system of laws and practices that provide a proper distribution of rights and opportunities for all citizens. The Bible does not lay out for us a detailed overview of the just ordering of a society. Instead, the biblical writers focus on groups of people whose legitimate cries for justice are often ignored.

The pages of Scripture refer several times to God's concerns for "widows and orphans." The social arrangement taken for granted in the Old and New Testament periods was patriarchy—the rule of adult males. Only men, for example, were allowed to give testimony in a court of law. If a wife or child had a legal claim to make, it would be up to the husband or father to take up their cause. Women and children were legally voiceless under those conditions. Widows and orphans, then, were very vulnerable because they had no adult male to take up their causes—no husbands or fathers. "Strangers in the land" were in a similar situation. They lacked legal status and could only be defended or protected if a Jewish adult male responded favorably to their concerns. God calls his people to take up the cause of victims of injustice, which certainly means addressing governments on their behalf. The prophet Daniel's urging to the wicked king of Babylon is a clear example of such an address: "Therefore, Your Majesty, be pleased to accept my advice: Renounce your sins by doing what is right, and your wickedness by being kind to the oppressed. It may be that then your prosperity will continue" (Daniel 4:27).

Second, the Bible also affirms the call for "domestic Tranquility" found in the preamble. The apostle Paul, when instructing his young friend Timothy regarding prayers on behalf of rulers, emphasizes that a key motivation should be our desire that "we may live peaceful and quiet lives in all godliness and holiness." The prophet Micah employed a compelling image when he envisioned a well-governed society, where all people "will sit under their own vine / and under their own fig tree, / and no one will make them afraid" (Micah 4:4).

The arrangement Micah calls for requires yet a third governmental function: for people to live with some measure of security, it is necessary for a government to "provide for the common defense," as the preamble expresses it. Governments establish and maintain police protection and military forces. This is the dimension of political authority that Paul refers to in Romans 13 as the power of "the sword." Under our sinful conditions, law-abiding citizens need to be protected against those who break the law within the nation while also receiving protection against external enemies.

Finally, the preamble highlights the state's calling to "promote the general Welfare." This is a broad assignment, and we also find it referred to in the psalmist's petition, that under a God-honoring government "the mountains bring prosperity to the people, / the hills the fruit of righteousness" (Psalm 72:3). Psalm 72 features an intriguing image in describing this general role of government in our collective lives. The writer prays that the laws and practices of the ruler will be "like rain falling on a mown field, / like showers watering the earth" (Psalm 72:6). The state has an obligation to ensure that we grow, that we flourish.

Several years ago, when I was studying the political views of seventeenth-century Scottish Presbyterian theologians, I found them referring often to those whom God calls to national political leadership as "nursing fathers."[1] One reason I found this image a bit puzzling was that these stern Calvinist thinkers were not typically given to gentle intimate-sounding formulations in dealing with political topics. This was a period in Scottish history when Presbyterians were engaged in considerable conflict with other faith groups in public life. They often used the term *abomination*, for example, in referring to Anglican or Catholic rulers.

In expressing their own political views, these Presbyterians also frequently depicted God as wanting Scotland—a "chosen nation," in their view—to conform to patterns much like those that characterized life in ancient Israel. Mixed in with their many statements about God's displeasure with how things were going in the Scottish nation were the occasional gentle references to the nurturing power of civil government. In exploring their biblical references in this regard, I discovered that the nursing image is found in only two verses in the Bible, both from the book of Isaiah: "Kings will be your foster fathers, / and their queens your nursing mothers" (Isaiah 49:23). "You will . . . be nursed at royal breasts" (Isaiah 60:16).

Obviously, neither of these verses would serve well as a biblical text to be featured on a congregation's website during an election season! But their point is a good one to keep in mind when we think about the purposes of government. Those old Presbyterian writers were insisting that God wants governments to nurture the citizens under their authority.

In attempting to apply to present-day United States what Old Testament passages have to say about government, we obviously have to acknowledge that we do not live in a monarchy. America has a more complex arrangement; our "king" actually consists of three equal branches of national government—the president and cabinet members, the Congress, and the courts. Even so, we need to think about what it means for this government to exhibit a nurturing spirit that cares about the well-being of all the people, with special attention to "the needy."

There is much to debate regarding what this means in terms of practical policy. I, for one, need those debates since I have changed my mind on policy matters many times in my adult life—and I continue to struggle with these matters in my own mind and heart.

THE "SIZE" QUESTION

When I have given class lectures and public talks on these biblical references to the tasks of government, questions typically come up about whether I am saying that the Bible calls for "big government."[2]

I am not a "big government" advocate. I know how a top-heavy governmental bureaucracy can become a detriment to the common good. When someone proposes that the government should provide a specific social service, it is important to ask whether what is being proposed might be more effectively provided by nongovernmental groups and agencies.

What I have been insisting on here is that Christians must think biblically about the role of governments in God's purposes for collective human life. And I do believe that the state exists as more than a remedy for our human sinfulness. To be sure, sin is real and it does need to be kept under control. Thus, the need for a police force, military protection, and criminal proceedings. But, as we have seen, the Bible also points us to more positive functions of government. Maintaining streets and highways also seems to be a necessary government service. Attention also must be given to public safety measures: parents whose kids walk to neighborhood schools should be grateful for stop signs, traffic lights, speed zones, and crossing guards.

I personally would add several other things to the list. I think public parks are important, as well as municipal museums, government archives, support for the arts—to name a few. I am also grateful for unelected civil servants who provide standard information about Social Security benefits, shelve books in city libraries, and serve as police radio dispatchers. And then there are the very lonely government employees: the folks who accept dangerous assignments as CIA and FBI agents or who stand guard at remote military outposts. I consider all of us to be blessed by laws preventing child and spousal abuse, as well as by consumer safety regulations.

But I find that it is at least as important to keep specifics of this sort in mind when people talk about "getting the government out of our lives." And even if we think that there are some things of this sort that a government should not do, I would still want to insist that a government is obliged at least to see to it that they are done by other entities.

For me, that distinction between what a government must itself do and what it must provide through other means in the public sector is one that calls for discernment. We need to make our choices in the light of what resources are available. Sometimes a government must step in to provide an important service simply because it would not be provided otherwise. This is what we mean by the state's maintenance of a "safety net" in some areas of genuine human need.

The Catholic tradition of social teachings sets forth a helpful guideline in this regard, in what it calls the Subsidiarity Principle. In short, this principle affirms that "higher" bodies should not do what can be done as well or better by "lower" bodies. This means, for example, that the federal government should defer to state governments in many areas, just as state authorities should stay out of providing services that could be accomplished efficiently by more local bodies. And it also means that public agencies should not do what can be done as well by nongovernmental bodies.

Note that I just stipulated that the state should not do for us what can be done "efficiently" and "as well" by entities in the private sector. Those are important considerations, and there are others that should also be mentioned. The great nineteenth-century Dutch Calvinist leader Abraham Kuyper was very concerned to define the limits of the state, and he was able to put many of his ideas on this into practice. While he was a brilliant theologian—many would say one of the great theological thinkers of his century—he led his party in the Dutch Parliament for several decades, and eventually served a term as the prime minister of the Netherlands.

Kuyper warned against the state becoming an "octopus" that would reach out with its tentacles to choke life out of businesses, families, art guilds, universities, and other spheres whose flourishing is essential to a rich cultural life. But Kuyper was aware that entities besides the state can also use tentacles to stifle life. Powerful families can oppose zoning laws that impinge on their own properties. Pharmaceutical companies can price their products in a way that drains the resources of needy patients. The ideologies of secularist scholars can come to exercise undue influence over public school curricula. In cases of that sort, Kuyper saw the state as having a special obligation to protect each of the diverse social institutions from being stifled by others. While he rightly worried about governments getting too "big," he also wanted the state to have the authority to protect us from other forms of "bigness."

I know that some of the examples I have mentioned here would not sit well with some of my fellow Christians. My reason for citing them is mainly just to have specific examples in mind. Too often we make sweeping claims about the dangers of "big government" because there is something that the state is doing that we do not like—but we don't think about what this means for instances where we want the government to play an active role.

PATRIOTIC PRAYING

Our understanding of the proper nature and limits of government is important for how we *pray* for those who govern us. Patriotic praying is also one of our obligations as Christian citizens. We have seen several biblical instances where we are commanded to pray to the Lord on behalf of those who exercise authority over us.

To be patriotic Christians, then, is to love our government in the right way, and this means being sure to pray for it. It is significant to remember, though, that while we are told to

pray for "all those in authority" (1 Timothy 2:2), the mandate
to do so is linked, as we have seen, to our nurturing a prayerful
concern for the well-being of the broader human community.
A worthy government is one that cares for the well-being of
all its citizens. This is an instance of what we have shown to
be a general biblical theme: submitting to those in power
cannot be divorced from our solidarity with all the human
beings whom those authorities are called to serve. We saw
this in Jeremiah's counsel to the ancient Jewish exiles. The
prophet clearly intended that they pray for the Babylonian
authorities; that was an implicit in his more general command
to the exiles that they were to "pray to the LORD" on behalf of
"the city to which I have carried you into exile," in fulfillment
of their obligation to seek the shalom of this place where the
Lord has led them (Jeremiah 29:7). The apostle Peter makes
the same point when he tells us that what we owe to the governing authorities is the same "proper respect" that we—and
they—owe to all our fellow citizens (1 Peter 2:17).

PRAYER AS POLITICAL ACTION

Political praying is a key element in our active citizenship. It
is *doing* something important. The idea that prayer is a form
of political action was impressed upon me in a forceful way
by a South African activist. When the apartheid system was
still in effect in that country, I helped to organize gatherings
to promote Christian awareness of the brutalities committed
against that nation's Black population. As a person of Dutch
Reformed convictions, I had personal reasons for trying to
make it clear that the theology associated with support for
apartheid was a distorted version of my theological tradition.

At one of those gatherings, I arranged for the group to hear from Motlalepula Chabaku, a Black Christian activist who was visiting the United States at the time. She delivered a spiritually stirring address to our group, focusing specifically on some measures that we could take to partner with her community's efforts to promote justice. At the end of her inspiring speech she urged us to keep praying for an end to *apartheid* policies.

In the discussion period following her talk a young man stood to register a concern about her call to prayer. He told her how much he appreciated all that she said but that it was dangerous to tell folks like us to pray for South Africa. "In the end, that's what we will take home from this experience. We will pray, and that will be it." And then he raised his voice and said in an anguished tone: "I'm sick of just praying about this. I want us to do something!"

Her response had a lasting impact on me. "I'm not recommending 'just praying,'" she responded gently. "I gave you a number of things that you should also be doing." But then she added: "Don't knock praying, though. Prayer is doing something. It is petitioning our sovereign God, who is the highest authority in the universe. This is an important kind of action!"

That was a powerful insight. Prayer is indeed an act of petitioning. And it is more. We can have conversations with God about the challenges of public life, including expressing to him our frustrations about why things are not going the way we think they should. The Hebrew psalms also include many prayers of lament—which is also "doing something." The Bible gives us permission to lodge our complaints with God: Where are you, Lord? Were you asleep when all of this was happening? Why are you silent when these horrible things are happening? How long before we can see the end of this?

But the young man was also right in insisting that "just praying" is not enough. We need to do other things as well in acting on our concerns for peace and justice and righteousness. God expects us to do more than pray. But not less.

THANKFUL PRAYING

Our prayers for government should also include expressions of gratitude. This may seem a bit of a stretch for some of us, given the much-discussed divisiveness these days in the halls of power. But it is important to think more broadly about the ways in which governments serve us.

I was made aware of the extent of those services when I was asked by a Christian group to write a prayer on their website for a series of daily devotionals about political life. I was one of several who were asked to write these prayers, and each of us was given a specific assignment. I was asked to focus on persons in government who were not elected to their positions. I did know, of course, that government is more than elected officials, but this assignment forced me to think about the range of services covered by this category. Flippant references to "government bureaucracies" and "the deep state" do not do justice to their contributions to our lives. The thousands of hardworking civil servants compose the infrastructure of the important workings of government.

Here is the prayer that I wrote:

You have commanded your people, O Lord, to pray for those in authority over us, and we do this by asking your blessing on all who have been elected to positions of influence in political life. To those prayers we add our petitions on behalf of those who have chosen to devote their careers to non-elective careers in civil service— those who sort and classify materials for governmental archives, those who interpret agricultural policies to rural constituents, those who answer phone inquiries, those who serve the cause of justice and peace in lonely and dangerous outposts—for these and for many others who work faithfully for the common good, we lift up our prayers. Give your special strength and wisdom to those who administer programs and policies that promote the well-being of widows and orphans; of strangers in the land; of the hungry, the homeless, the abused, and those who live in poverty. Through all these efforts may your kingdom come and your will be done, on earth as it is in heaven. Through Jesus Christ our Lord. Amen.

After submitting this prayer for the website, I wished I had mentioned the kind of government service that a woman named Marnie performed. When I called the local Department of Motor Vehicles to request information that I needed, I was put on hold for over ten minutes, forced to listen to bad music that was frequently interrupted by a recorded voice telling me how much my call was appreciated. When a "live" voice finally came on, I was in an irritable mood, which I did not hide from the person I was talking to. She identified herself as Marnie, and she offered a friendly apology for my having to wait, and then she patiently answered my questions. When she was sure that I had what I needed, she signed off in a kind voice: "Okay, Richard, and I do hope that you have a bless-ed day!"

Reflecting on that conversation, I made a vow to myself, and to God, that the next time I had the assignment as a visiting preacher to offer the congregational prayer, I would say something I had never heard before in a worship service. In praying for "the powers that be," I would find a way to thank the Lord for the people who answer the phones at the Department of Motor Vehicles!

SIX

LEARNING FROM ARGUMENTS

heocracy is for many people a no-no word these days, and
I understand why. It is often applied to contemporary societies where everything is under the control of a specific religious perspective, and persons who are not adherents to that
faith are forced to conform—or worse yet, are persecuted.

Among Christians, though, the word is not always used in
a disparaging way. Theologians will remind us that much of
the laws and practices prescribed in the Old Testament were
meant to be applicable to a theocracy, in which the people of
Israel rightly saw themselves as being governed in accordance
with the revealed will of God. Typically, theologians explain
that arrangement to make it clear that things are very different in present-day democratic societies, where religious
freedoms, along with the right to profess no religious faith at
all, are guaranteed by law. I support that pluralistic approach.
I have no interest in taking the theocratic system of laws of
ancient Israel and implementing it in today's society.

There is one important sense, however, in which I see the
word *theocracy* as signifying something central to our faith as
Christians. *Theocracy* literally means "the rule of God," and the

Bible teaches that God does rule over the whole creation. The psalmist tells us that "the earth is the LORD's, and everything in it, / the world, and all who live in it" (Psalm 24:1). And the apostle Paul adds the important information that Jesus Christ is "the head over every power and authority" on the earth (Colossians 2:10). Everything that exists is under God's rule. That *is* theocracy! And our conviction that we live in a theocratically arranged universe is the source of meaning and hope for believers in the deepest places of our being.

ACTIVE PATIENCE

Having made that important point about God's theocratic rule over all things, I have to emphasize that I do *not* believe that we should work to change our political system from a democracy to a theocracy. I fully support living in a democratic republic. Why do I believe that this is the kind of political system American Christians should fully support? For starters, we begin with the obvious point that not everyone acknowledges the theocratic nature of reality. There are large numbers of our fellow human beings who do not recognize the God of the Bible as the sovereign Ruler of the universe. What we hope for, then, is that these people will come to understand the claims of the gospel and freely offer their lives of service to the Lord. This is why we must support the work of evangelism, inviting people to come to know Jesus as the only true Lord and Savior.

It is this emphasis on freely offering our obedience to God that has important implications for our understanding of political matters. The Old Testament writers make it clear over and over again that the Lord is not pleased by a grudging conformity to his commands: "For I desire mercy, not sacrifice, / and acknowledgment of God rather than burnt offerings" (Hosea 6:6). We do not serve God's purposes in the world by forcing people to submit to "Christian" laws, against their own values and convictions.

Furthermore, we should cultivate a spirit of toleration regarding the range of permissible behaviors in our society. Not everything that can be judged to be sinful ought to be made illegal. While I don't like the blasphemous language that I hear all too frequently these days in the movies that I watch, I am not inclined to call for legal bans on these expressions.

I like a phrase that I learned from some Mennonite friends. We are "living in the time of God's patience." Someday the sovereign rule of God will be revealed to all people, when Jesus returns to make all things new. In the meantime, we live in the awareness that God is being patient with widespread unbelief in the world.

GENUINE ENGAGEMENT

When I first started studying Christian political thought as a college student, I remember being given by one of my professors a decidedly "necessary evil" perspective on American democracy. Our democratic system, he argued, is really not very good—but it does have the virtue of not being quite as bad as any of the alternatives. Our system manages, he said, to prevent a large number of sinful people committed to their own selfish purposes from doing as much harm to each other as they otherwise would.

I found that viewpoint to be a bit of a downer. I wanted something more positive. And over the years I have come to cherish some valuable aspects of our diverse culture in America, as well as our way of going about the tasks of governing ourselves.

There is no need for me to go into academic detail here about the merits and demerits of the American political system. We Christians can foster a healthy spirit of patriotism without each citizen being required to grasp the philosophical basics of democratic theory. I do want to emphasize, however, that we ought to celebrate the benefits of living our lives as citizens in the kind of diverse culture that we experience in the United States.

The key to appreciating these benefits is a willingness to learn from persons who are different from us. And it is important to emphasize here that this includes learning from folks with whom we have quite serious disagreements— different religious convictions, opposition to religious beliefs as such, or diverse moral lifestyles.

What can we learn in a context where that kind of diversity is present? For one thing, we can learn about our own mistakes and misdeeds. It is important to acknowledge that we do need to look to folks who disagree with us to help us with this kind of learning.

In the 1970s there were many reports about "Christian/ Marxist dialogue" going on in Latin America. These reports did not play well in the United States, Canada, and the United Kingdom. (In parts of Western Europe, though, there was considerably more openness to the idea.) At the time, I shared some of the doubts expressed by the critics. I was teaching political philosophy courses, and I wanted my students to see the obvious differences between Christian and Marxist thought. Besides, in reality the Marxism of the Soviet Union was clearly a horribly oppressive system for millions of people.

During that time, however, the great Anglican leader John Stott—a hero to so many of us in the evangelical world—made a bold move. He invited a Protestant theologian from Argentina, José Míguez Bonino, to present some lectures about his participation in that dialogue to an evangelical audience in London. The book based on those lectures, *Christians and Marxists: The Mutual Challenge to Revolution*, taught me some important lessons. Míguez Bonino clearly rejected, for example, the Marxists' insistence that religion is an oppressive force in human affairs. At the same time, he acknowledged that some of the Marxists' examples of religion's bad influences are legitimate, and he insisted that is important to admit these misuses of religious convictions. But does that mean, Míguez Bonino asked, that we are ultimately accountable to our secular critics? Only the Lord is our judge. But while our critics cannot sit in judgment over us, he said, we do need to allow them, in the presence of that Lord, to take the witness stand in order to present their evidence against us.[1]

I began to take that seriously in my own encounters with folks with whom I disagree on basic issues. In welcoming them to the witness stand, I have learned much in the process. A gay man informed me, angrily but convincingly, about the abusive language religious conservatives like me have used to condemn him. A rabbi told me about being bullied and called a "Christ killer" by Christian schoolmates at a time when he was the only Jewish kid in his school. Those stories, and many more, have taught me much about how believers like me are often seen by people with whom we disagree. Necessary lessons!

RECEIVING TRUTHS

Bob Lane is one of my favorite dialogue partners on some significant theological topics. I got to know him during his nine years as CEO of the John Deere Company, and we continue our discussions now that he is retired. Our relationship got started when he contacted me to discuss something I had written about the theological basis for believing that Christians can learn positive truths from non-Christians on important topics. Bob had been fleshing out his own theological convictions on this subject ever since he had taken a philosophy course at Wheaton College. His teacher, Arthur Holmes, had impressed on his students the profound claim that Holmes also chose as the title for one of his books: that "all truth is God's truth."

The John Deere Company is a large international corporation, and Bob worked with a team of key managers who represented a wide variety of religious and worldview perspectives: Muslims, Hindus, Confucianists, Christians, Jews, persons who claimed no religious faith at all, and many others. Bob did not just tolerate this diversity; he relished it. The opportunity to learn from others was for him a blessing from the Lord. But he was also saddened by the way that many of his fellow Christians were more inclined to adopt an us-versus-them posture toward non-Christians. So he was eager to engage in some theological reflection on these matters.

I won't go into the technical theological details on this here, but the subject that brought the two of us together has a long and distinguished history in the Christian tradition, drawing on schools of thought that feature some key theological themes about how believers and unbelievers can find common ground in the areas of truth and morality: general revelation, natural theology, moral law, common grace.

Needless to say, Christian theologians have also wrestled with how to reconcile or combine these themes with the fact of human fallenness. Sin has entered the world because of our rebellion against the will of God, and this does seriously affect the ways that sinful people think, feel, and act in dealing with the deepest concerns of the human spirit. That is an important reality in our shared lives as human beings, and it cannot be ignored by Christians. But neither can we ignore the continuing presence of the realities of sin in our own lives. We need to open ourselves to people who can remind us of our own prejudices, inconsistencies, and misdeeds.

Our shared fallenness continues to affect our individual and collective lives in profound ways. We Christians are not exempt from the struggle with sin in our own souls. A self-righteous spirit should have no place in our relations with others. But there is another factor that should keep us humble as we engage with people whose beliefs differ from our own: we are finite creatures. Even if sin could be completely banished from our lives, we would still need to be learners. It was this eagerness to learn that Bob Lane took into meetings with Muslim John Deere dealers in Pakistan and with regional government officials in rural China. Effective business leaders should always be open to discovering new insights from others about stewardship, promoting the human good, healthy employee practices, and the like.

John Calvin is often portrayed as having a thoroughly pessimistic view about the capacities of fallen human beings, but as a law student he had learned much from ancient

Greco-Roman writers such as Cicero and Seneca. He continued to acknowledge their wisdom after his evangelical conversion. "If we regard the Spirit of God as the sole fountain of truth," Calvin wrote, "we shall neither reject the truth itself, nor despise it where it shall appear, unless we wish to dishonor the Spirit of God."[2] Calvin would encourage us to stay open to receiving truths from our non-Christian neighbors in the public arena today.

"LEFT" AND "RIGHT"

In renewing my registration as a California voter, I was asked on the form for my political affiliation. I intended to identify as independent, but then I noticed that one of the choices listed was American Independent Party, and I did not want to be seen as claiming that affiliation. So I wrote in the available box for comments that I do not want to be linked to any political party.

That is, of course, a personal choice that I would not prescribe for all Christians. In 2018 Pastor Tim Keller wrote a wise opinion piece for the *New York Times* with the title "How Do Christians Fit into the Two-Party System? They Don't."[3] I agree with Keller's answer. Of course some Christians do find it necessary to align with a specific party. They may be running for office, or they may form a strategic alliance over an issue of public policy. But, says Keller, we should never simply identify our Christian political perspective with the agenda of one of the existing parties. Our situation, he observes, is not unlike that of Joseph and Daniel in the Bible. They served in pagan governments, but they clearly refused to endorse everything that was expected of them by those determining policies.

I find it impossible to characterize my own political views as either left or right. I align with the conservative side of the social-political spectrum on some key issues while I move over to the other side on other topics. That general pattern strikes me as rather common among Christians. Even friends of mine who identify closely with the platform of one of the parties will admit in private conversation that theirs is not an across-the-board agreement.

Moreover, as Pastor Keller observes, "most political positions are not matters of biblical command but of practical wisdom."[4] Biblical teaching about God's concern for the poor and the oppressed does not provide us with clear counsel about welfare policies or mail-in ballots in national elections. We can be strongly supportive of "pro-life" principles while arguing with each other about how best to put those principles into action. People who are deeply committed to truth telling can also support espionage efforts in international relations.

The depiction of politics as the art of compromise is widely taken for granted. In distinctively Christian terms we might say that politics is the art of discernment. Christians are called to "live as children of light," affirming "all goodness, righteousness and truth." But this requires the practical work of exercising the gift of discernment, as we try to "find out what pleases the Lord" on complex matters (Ephesians 5:8-10).

Biblically faithful discernment does not take place in isolation. It is a communal activity. Together we seek the will of God on the challenges we face: praying together, in dialogue with each other, even—and perhaps, most importantly—arguing together. I use the verb *argue* in this regard with the views of G. K. Chesterton in mind. He was one of the great defenders of the faith in the early twentieth century, having converted to Catholicism after years as an atheist. Chesterton loved to argue, and he held that activity in high regard. There are too many quarrels in the world, Chesterton said, and people quarrel because they do not know how to argue. His great line on the subject was: "Perhaps the principal objection to a quarrel is that it interrupts an argument."[5]

To use Chesterton's distinction, we live in an era of much public quarreling but very little arguing. Legislative bodies engage in continuing partisan attacks. TV panelists yell at each other. Online forums feature nasty name-calling. One citizen's sign of hope is another citizen's conspiracy. Lecturers on university campuses are drowned out by protesters.

We desperately need arguments—and not just because respectful disagreements are "nice" but because they are crucial to the health of the human spirit. Our faith communities can provide alternative models, as in the song "They'll Know We Are Christians by Our Love."[6] But often what we do show others is just more quarreling.

I have no business allowing myself to come across as condescending on this problem. While I have written much about "convicted civility"—respecting others without compromising firm Christian convictions—I do not always live up to my ideals. I often pray the lines of my favorite come-to-Jesus hymn:

> Just as I am—though toss'd about
> With many a conflict, many a doubt,
> Fightings and fears within, without,
> O Lamb of God, I come![7]

All I can do is invite others to join me in praying that kind of prayer. Doing so is a way of admitting that we have a problem in the deep places of our own souls—a step in the right direction. Another step might be to enlist a fellow Christian who sees key issues differently as a dialogue partner for learning how to argue. This can be facilitated by learning about that person's personal journey. All of this is not only good for our own souls, it is good for the honoring service that we owe to the larger human community.

SEVEN

PATRIOTISM IN CHURCH

When a reporter was interviewing me about the interfaith dialogues in which I have been actively engaged, she asked me to identify my most difficult dialogues about religious matters. My answer: debates with fellow evangelical Christians. I experience a lot of quarreling in the Christian community and—to use G. K. Chesterton's distinction again—not enough arguing. While the Christian community should be a good place for us to process our differing views about how we can best serve our nation, experience teaches us that those conversations frequently go badly.

Actually, that is not surprising when it comes to patriotic topics. Our disagreements on many of these matters are not merely academic. They have serious practical implications. I can have a passionate argument with a non-Christian friend about how best to work for political change, and we can end the discussion by agreeing to disagree. It is different, however, when our differences are about what is going to happen next week in church when we gather to worship the Lord. The unique frustration over intra-Christian differences is what often goes on when we debate about how patriotic symbols and expressions may or may not be included within the worshiping life of the church.

WORSHIPING WHERE WE ARE

"Well, I made it through worship on Memorial Day weekend," Doug, a pastor friend, said to me. "Now I have to start worrying about the Fourth of July!" Doug resents the fact that his parishioners expect patriotic themes to be featured in worship around the time of major civic holidays. He does not like having to make reference to those matters in his prayers and sermons. And he finds much in the patriotic songs that are sung on such occasions to be theologically defective.

But it isn't just the special occasions that vex him. There is a national flag on permanent display in the sanctuary of his church, and he finds that offensive. He sees the flag posing a temptation to engage in "idolatry." It represents "civil religion"—which for him means the misusing of religious ideas to posit too close a relationship between "God and country"—and has no place, Doug says, in a sacred space devoted to the worship of the true God.

There are some things in Doug's outlook on patriotism in worship that I agree with, but I find it helpful for my thinking on these topics to debate with him. I am inclined to take a less harsh position on some of the matters he complains about so by pushing him to clarify for me what he really is concerned about, I can check out my own views and motives.

Doug certainly has no objection to including expressions of national concerns in worship services. For one thing, he regularly prays for our national leaders. But beyond that, he is clearly convinced that patriotic symbols and expressions have no place in Christian worship. In initially setting forth his view in one of our conversations, he gave the impression that he believes that a Christian worship service should in no way reflect the national setting in which it takes place. He likes the idea that, as he put it, if a Christian family from Ireland were to visit his congregation, they would be able to identify basically with all that happens in the worship service.

In our extended discussion, I pushed back, pointing out that on purely practical grounds it seems unrealistic to expect that visitors from one country will feel completely at home in a service in another country. One obvious factor is that they might not understand some colloquial phrases, and surely there will also be practices and modes of spiritual expression that differ from culture to culture.

Doug immediately acknowledged my point so I went a step further and appealed to a general concern that I know he is passionate about: cultural diversity. Isn't honoring our particular contexts in worship, I asked, actually a way of honoring God's own love of the diversity in his world? Christian worship is not a one-size-fits-all kind of thing. A worship service in Nigeria will be different from one in rural China. And in our own American communities we expect that worship at a retirement home will not be the same as one at a summer youth camp—to say nothing of how race and ethnicity shape our various worshiping patterns.

Doug acknowledged all of that, but he drew the line at expressions of citizenship loyalties in church. A family from another country should not have to encounter an American flag in church or put up with the singing of American patriotic songs.

Again I pushed back, asking him how would he react if he attended a worship service in an African nation that had just achieved independence after a long period of colonial rule, with the new national flag proudly on display in the sanctuary. Wouldn't it be likely that Christian citizens would want to be a positive Christian influence in this exciting time of nation building and that their worship might be directed toward thanksgiving to God for these new opportunities? And can't the American flag in our own churches serve to remind *us* that we need to wrestle with questions about what it means for us to be Christian citizens of *our* nation, the United States?

Doug thought for a moment and then replied that he could see my point. Maybe, he said, it would be okay for the flag to be in the African sanctuary for a Sunday celebrating new beginnings for the nation. Then the flag could be a focus for that congregation's reflections on what it means for them to serve the cause of Christ's kingdom in these new conditions as citizens of their nation. But to make the national flag a permanent fixture in Christian worship—in their setting or in ours—opens us up to "the temptation of nationalistic pride."

THE TEACHING TASK

I should admit at this point that I do not like it when a writer uses a discussion with another person to show how effective the writer was in revealing the other person's confusions. It may seem like that is what I have done in reporting my conversation with Doug, but that is not the whole story. I felt the strength of his convictions on the subject, and in our back and forth I was trying out ideas with Doug, adjusting my own views as we went along together. So, while I was happy, for example, when Doug agreed that a national flag can function as a visual aid in explicitly challenging us to wrestle with Christian questions about citizenship, I was still a little uneasy about what I was arguing for. I am well aware that a national flag has a sacred "feel" to it. It is not—or at least it should never be considered to be—a mere decoration. How, then, do we use its presence as a teaching aid without allowing its symbolic strength to detract from our focus on the absolute holiness of the God who calls us to worship him?

I acknowledged my misgivings about this to Doug, admitting that it would be wrong simply to assume that a national flag has a rightful place in our worshiping spaces. I told Doug that he was right to worry about the real danger that patriotic symbols and themes in worship can seriously detract from our focus on pledging our supreme allegiance to Christ and his kingdom. This is especially important to think carefully about in our American context where we regularly see ourselves competing with other large countries for prestige, economic power, and military superiority. In this sense we are not on a level playing field with small countries who have just broken free from colonial rule.

Again, though, none of this should be taken to mean that references to patriotism are simply inappropriate in an American church setting. On the contrary, they can provide important teaching opportunities about our genuinely Christian duties as citizens of the nations where the Lord calls us to serve the cause of his kingdom. But how does a congregation go about that teaching and learning?

Indeed, the teaching and learning aspects are especially relevant when patriotic displays and expressions are already in place. Doug's frustrations were due in part to realities that he had inherited when he arrived in this pastorate. The flag was already there in the sanctuary. The congregation had long taken it for granted that civic holidays would be acknowledged in planning worship services. And it is unlikely that these things came about by official decisions where, for example, a congregational meeting once voted to bring a flag into the sanctuary. No organist or choir director or worship team was ever hired primarily for the purpose of bringing more patriotism into the weekly services. Nor can a pastor who is unhappy about all of this propose that now a vote has to be taken to reverse these patterns. In this kind of situation, pastors and other church leaders need to reflect carefully on how to engage with expectations, patterns, and practices that have long existed. More specifically, they should find ways to turn these realities into opportunities.

For Doug to push for the flag to be removed, and for him to refuse to participate in, say, the honoring of military veterans in the congregation on Memorial Day weekend, could possibly bring about the end of his pastorate. It is much preferable to acknowledge the teaching opportunities presented by what has long been a part of the congregation's life.

A student once told me that for as long as he could remember his home congregation had always had a national flag in the sanctuary. "It fits the God-and-country perspective in our church," he said. "People just take it for granted that the American flag belongs there!" I asked him how he thought his pastor felt about the patriotic displays. The young man replied: "He has never said anything about it so I don't know for sure. But my guess is that he would rather not have the flag there."

I think that not saying anything about it is a failure in the church's teaching ministry. Here is how it could go differently. On a given civic holiday weekend service a pastor could point to the national flag and talk about the fact that it is a reminder that we are citizens of a specific nation and that we don't leave our citizenship roles and our patriotic affections at the door when we enter the church building for worship. It is a good thing to acknowledge that the Lord has given each of us a national setting in which to live. Christian citizenship is a good and important calling.

Having said that, the pastor could also say that our respect for the flag should not distract us from our ultimate allegiance to Jesus Christ. He or she could go on to point out that our worship services provide us with opportunities to become more aware of who we are as the elect people of God. We are citizens of our nation, but in our worship we acknowledge a higher citizenship—in the worldwide kingdom in which we have been incorporated by divine grace. Our supreme Ruler calls us to serve him in the broad and complex patterns of our lives.

Then the teaching could continue to point out that sometimes Christians seem more excited by our national identities than by our kingdom citizenship. There can be something seductive about patriotic sentiments. Symbols often play a special role in this seductiveness. For many Americans, for example, the flag is not only a symbol of our ideals of freedom and justice; it also stands in their minds for wartime victories that impose our national will on other peoples. Our flag has led us into battles. We raised it over territories that previously belonged to other tribes and nations. The flag can be associated in our hearts and minds with having a divine destiny to be a conquering force in the world. The temptations are spiritual in nature, and they should be countered, and not encouraged, in our worshiping lives. Being in church should make us aware that we are asked to give our ultimate loyalty to the one supreme Ruler, a Lord who calls us to pursue justice in ways that honor him as the Prince of Peace.

THE PLACEMENT OF FLAGS

My discussion of flags in church has focused here on flags in congregational sanctuaries, but that does not exhaust the topics of national flags in Christian contexts. Take the example of evangelical colleges, universities, and seminaries. It is a matter of law in the United States that any educational institution that receives federal funding must display the national flag on its campus. These schools are typically quite dependent on federal funds: their tuition income relies in significant ways on student federal loans. Faculty members receive research grants from federal agencies, such as the National Science Foundation and the National Endowment for the Humanities.

Even apart from that regulation, the flag is typically on display in college stadiums and gymnasiums, where athletic events regularly begin with the singing or playing of the national anthem. And, for that matter, congregational facilities are often more than sanctuaries. Many local churches these days refer to their building complexes as "campuses," with administrative centers, gymnasiums, libraries, church education rooms, and the like.

Questions about the presence of a national flag in those diverse settings are less controversial than the issue of having a flag in a place specifically devoted to worship. To recognize this is, it seems to me, to clarify what is essential to discussions of the flag in church.

PATRIOTIC SINGING

Back now to the worship setting. If a congregation is given to singing patriotic songs in worship—at least on special occasions—these too can serve as teaching tools. Many of these songs make passing theological references that can fit nicely in a sermon on some important topic. One patriotic hymn declares that God is the "Author of Liberty."[1] That has implications for people who say that they are free to make their own choices however they want.

Or consider the prayer song: "God bless America, land that I love / Stand beside her and guide her / Through the night with the light from above."[2] As believers who acknowledge to God that "Your Word is a lamp for my feet, / a light on my path" (Psalm 119:105), what guidance does this "light from above" give us for the paths that we walk as citizens who want the Lord truly to bless our nation?

Here I need to tell a story about my own struggles in learning how to use a particular patriotic song as a teaching tool. The song is "America the Beautiful," which has more theological content than simply a couple of passing references to God. The verses that make up the song were originally written as a poem by Katharine Lee Bates, who published it in 1893 in a Congregationalist magazine. Two years later her words were put to music.

The standard version of the song has four verses, and my focus has been on the final verse, where Bates looks to a glorious future for the American nation:

O beautiful for patriot dream
That sees beyond the years

Thine alabaster cities gleam
Undimmed by human tears!
America! America!
God shed his grace on thee,
And crown thy good with brotherhood
From sea to shining sea![3]

My personal history of thinking about the theology expressed in this verse has significance for me because my first effort at speaking about it publicly put me in an awkward situation in a speech to a large audience. As it turned out, however, my experience of awkwardness was formative for how I have come to think about patriotic themes.

In 1976 I was invited by an evangelical school to give several lectures on faith and citizenship. My talks were planned as a part of the school's bicentennial celebration of the nation's founding. The first three of my presentations were academic lectures to the campus community. The fourth and final event, though, would be a little different. It was to be an evening gathering, a public bicentennial celebration, to be attended by members of a number of local evangelical congregations. It would be a fairly large crowd, I was told, and my address should be "more of a popular inspirational kind of talk."

I prepared this public talk carefully, writing out extensive notes. What I wanted to emphasize was how the United States had indeed been blessed by God in significant ways during the two hundred years of its history, while I would also point to the need for Christian citizens to think biblically about how we serve our country in a God-honoring manner.

In illustrating how our love of our country could be paired with our desire to call the nation to conform to God's standards of public righteousness, I decided to use the fourth verse of "America the Beautiful" as an example. I would point out that in writing this verse Katharine Lee Bates was borrowing several images from Revelation 21 and 22. There the apostle sees a vision of the new Jerusalem, the glorious Holy City that descends from the heavens at the end time. The city's streets are bedecked with precious metals and jewels. In this city the Lord God will wipe away all tears from the eyes of those who enter the gates. And the leaves of the Tree of Life will bring healing to the nations of the earth.

In drawing on these biblical motifs in her poem, Katharine Lee Bates applied them directly to America. The urban centers of the United States, she said, will become "alabaster cities" where human life will flourish "undimmed by human tears." Harmony and peace will spread over America "from sea to shining sea."

My intention was to suggest—gently—to the audience that we have to be very careful about using biblical references to portray the United States as uniquely blessed by God. In the Bible it is the people of Israel who are designated as a chosen nation—a status given to the ancient Israelites to highlight God's call to them to show the rest of the nations what it means for a people in their corporate life "to act justly and to love mercy and to walk humbly with your God" (Micah 6:8). And, as I pointed out in an earlier chapter, when in the New Testament the apostle Peter uses this same language of collective chosenness, he applies it directly to the church: "But you are a chosen people, a royal priesthood, a holy nation, God's special possession" (1 Peter 2:9).

To repeat my earlier point: chosenness in the Bible is not granted to a present-day nation like the United States. In the Old Testament, Israel was chosen by God to be his unique people: "I will also make you a light for the Gentiles, / that my salvation may reach to the ends of the earth" (Isaiah 49:6). In the New Testament this status has been extended to the church as the redeemed people of God, drawn from many races and nations. This is the apostle Peter's point in the passage just quoted. We as a multinational Christian community are a collection of individuals who once were not a people but by God's grace have become God's people, called to serve God's purposes in the world.

I knew that it would not be very effective if I was too harsh in criticizing Katharine Lee Bates's verse, in which the clear impression is given that there is a special status for the United States in God's plan for the nations. But I was convinced that her depiction of a transformed future America was theologically problematic. In writing her poem in the 1890s, she was influenced by a climate in American culture of optimism about the future. A key influence in this was the recent emergence of Darwinian evolutionary thought, which fostered the notion that humanity was evolving toward higher achievements. Many theologians were influenced by this mood, and they saw American society in particular as being prepared by God for some significant new blessings in the century that was about to begin. America would lead the way, they argued, in moving toward a fuller manifestation of the kingdom of God on earth with the arrival of new manifestations of widespread peace and justice.

In my planned speech I was going to address this historical context of her poem and point out that we can now see how misguided this optimism was. The twentieth century was to see America involved in the two world wars and in major conflicts in Korea and Vietnam. The horrors of the Holocaust would occur, and the Middle East would suffer from seemingly unsolvable tensions. On the domestic front racial conflict would increase, and serious signs of damage to our natural environment would emerge. If we Christians are going to be optimistic about the future, it cannot be because of trust in a gradual progress toward better days. We must base our hope in God's ultimate victory over the very real powers of evil—powers that continue to threaten the well-being of the American nation. Christians need to be on guard for when those influences come to shape the nation's life.

When the evening arrived, the school's auditorium was filled. As I sat on the platform waiting for my time to speak, I was nervous, but I also felt well prepared with my extensive notes in hand. During the first part of the program there were some dramatic readings about the United States' founding events and some choral presentations. Then a local evangelical leader stepped to the podium to introduce me as guest speaker for the occasion.

He gave a friendly introduction and was about to call me to the podium when suddenly he paused. Then this: "You know, Dr. Mouw is going to speak to us this evening about how God has blessed our great nation. And I think that it would be great before he speaks for us to stand and sing together the words of that great song, 'America the Beautiful.' Let's sing the first verse and then also that wonderful verse about how the 'patriot dream' shows us that there are even greater blessings yet to come for our beloved country!"

Then the audience rose to sing—a cappella and with great fervor. And I sang too, all the while experiencing some panic. I knew that I could not simply go ahead with what I had planned to say about the song these folks were singing. I was going to have to revise on my feet.

And revise I did. I still quoted the "patriot dream" verse, pointing out that Bates was using biblical imagery in looking forward to the time when the Lord would bring the full blessings of the kingdom to all who have put their faith in Jesus Christ. But then I also quoted some lines from the second verse of the Bates song:

> America! America!
> God mend thine every flaw,
> Confirm thy soul with self-control,
> Thy liberty in law![4]

As Christians, I said, we know that God will only bless us as individuals and as a nation if we confess our flaws and plead for healing so that God can mend us for active obedience to his will. And it is this active obedience that is our real civic duty as disciples of Jesus Christ.

My speech seemed to be well received. And, as I said earlier, I came to see the experience as formative for my further thinking about issues relating to patriotism.

USING BATES POSITIVELY

So, how did that experience influence my continuing views about these matters? And how does that influence figure into what I now want to say about Christians and patriotism? I think the influence will be obvious as I move along in my discussion, but a few thoughts here might be helpful.

As I reflect on that experience, two things stand out for me. One is that, for all of the awkwardness of the moment for me, I was glad that I joined in the singing that night. I felt the fervor of the audience as they sang the words of Katharine Lee Bates's song. More important, I sensed that their passion was an expression of legitimate patriotic sentiments. These were followers of Jesus Christ who were also expressing their love for their nation.

Of course, there likely was also some lack of clarity at play in the singing about how to relate faith in God to love of country. But this would not have been the right occasion simply to offer some critical thoughts about how Bates had used biblical imagery. Yes, Bates herself was caught up in enthusiasm for the idea of progress. And yes, we can now see, from the vantage point of knowing what actually happened in subsequent years, that this optimism was seriously misguided. But does that mean that on this occasion I should have focused on how her verse about the future of America was somewhat misguided theologically?

No. In fact, in retrospect I think it would have been good for me to be the one who requested that we sing Bates's song that evening. The very fact that it is nicely crafted as poetry and highly singable in its musical form makes it appropriate to single out for what it says that can inspire a proper kind of Christian perspective on citizenship.

Here are the positive points I would want to get across to that audience about Bates's message. We sing this song about America because it is the land where the Lord has placed us. And we sing it as citizens who know we have a responsibility to act on our expressions of hope for the future that God has promised to people and to nations who honor his purposes for human beings.

But, I would point out, Bates is not just telling us that we are on our way to a glorious future. There is more to her message, especially as captured in two of her themes. One is that we cannot flourish as a nation if we fail to acknowledge our sinfulness: "America! America! God mend thine every flaw." We Christians know that as individuals we cannot expect God's blessings unless we confess our very real sins. And this is true in our collective lives also, where our flaws are very real. Not only are our streets not paved with gold right now, but our cities are plagued with poverty and injustice. Our "fruited plain" is threatened by environmental degradation. The promise of human unity is at best a distant hope.

As believers, then, we can lead the way in honestly facing our national misdeeds and shortcomings. To pray for a beautiful America is to show a spirit of national humility and repentance.

Bates's second theme is the celebration of the realities of divine mercy: "America! America! God shed his grace on thee." Because our country is not innately better than other countries, to the degree that we are blessed among the nations it is because we have been committed to principles and values that we have been empowered to pursue because of God's merciful dealings with us. We Christians know this in our personal lives, and we are obligated to proclaim it in our witness to our nation as well. We can acknowledge that we cannot bring the full blessings of Bates's vision by our own efforts—it is a dream about what we know will come in the end only by God's abundant grace toward those who have been convicted of their sinful flaws.

EIGHT

RELIGION IN PUBLIC LIFE?

Using G. K. Chesterton's distinction again, we have a "quarreling" problem in contemporary public life, and I have been urging us as Christians to model a different way of engaging our differences. I have also urged us to begin cultivating this different way by starting in our own souls so that we can show others it is possible to treat each other with respect, even when our disagreements are serious.

Our present-day polarizations may be more pronounced than in the past, but the problem itself has been there since America's beginning. James Madison, one of America's Founding Fathers, expressed his worry about this in The Federalist Papers, which he coauthored with Alexander Hamilton. Madison posed the question of how a properly functioning government should deal with the presence of "factions"— partisan groups whose activities pose a threat to civil society. And he specifically mentioned "zeal for different opinions concerning religion" as one of the factors that "divided mankind into parties, inflamed them with mutual animosity, and rendered them much more disposed to vex and oppress each other than to co-operate for their common good."[1]

Madison had it right. Religion has frequently been a destructive force in human affairs. And it certainly continues to be so in our American context. However, it does not have to be that way.

POLITICAL USES OF RELIGIOUS BELIEFS

I have already discussed ways in which our religious convictions as Christians can inspire and strengthen our roles as citizens, and I have emphasized the importance of talking with others about our Christian convictions. But what about those public contexts where our gatherings are meant to affirm and reinforce our shared commitments as citizens? To stress the unique teachings of the Christian faith would go against the intended purposes of such occasions, but there is a long tradition in America of expressing religious ideas and themes in public life that are stated in more "generic" terms than our specifically Christian convictions. How should we view such things?

This is no hypothetical question. These more generic religious expressions abound in our national culture. The Declaration of Independence states that we are "endowed by [our] Creator with certain unalienable Rights." Our Pledge of Allegiance describes us as a nation "under God." We sing about God blessing America. We have invocations at city council meetings. Our presidents annually call for a national day of thanksgiving. Our armed forces employ clergy as military chaplains.

All of this falls under the label of *civil religion*. That term gets used in different ways in American life, but basically it refers to the use of religious language and symbols to reinforce respect for the role of government in our lives. In the practices I just mentioned—prayers at major public events, for example— the expressions are broadly thought of as Judeo-Christian, although there is nothing in them that would rule out Muslim assent. This generic character is seen as necessary to civil religion. And it is precisely this lack of specificity that leads some Christian thinkers to oppose civil religion—accusing it of using pious sentiments to serve the government's purposes.

That concern is understandable. The view that religion can serve the aims of government has a long history. For example, when Plato argued in his great dialogue *The Republic* that societies should be ruled by philosopher-kings, he realized that ordinary citizens would not be inclined simply to accept what gets decided by intellectuals who formulate laws that they discover by using reason to contemplate the ideals of justice. Consequently, Plato argued that the common folks should be taught that the gods required this arrangement.[2]

Similarly, in the eighteenth century, Jean Jacques Rousseau—generally acknowledged to be the first political theorist to set forth a philosophical account of civil religion— argued that being a true citizen required the setting aside of one's own individual desires in favor of conforming to what he labeled "the General Will." But, realizing how difficult it is for naturally self-centered persons to be transformed into altruistic citizens, Rousseau proposed a simple set of religious beliefs that people should be required to accept on pain of death: one, a belief in an all-powerful God; second, the conviction that in the life hereafter those who served the General Will would be rewarded and those who had disobeyed would be punished; and, third, reverence for "the sanctity of the social contract and the laws."[3]

There is good reason to think that neither Plato nor Rousseau personally embraced those religious teachings. They were proposing that religious language can be useful for the efforts by political authorities to enforce their policies and laws.

That approach strikes me as a cynical way of using religious ideas in public life, but that does not mean that I reject the content of those beliefs. Rousseau's list, for example, is composed of some basic Christian teachings: the existence of a God who calls us to live righteous lives, the reality of heaven and hell, and the sanctity of promoting human community ordered by just laws. We need to ensure, though, that these true teachings are put to uses that serve God's purposes in human life.

PROMOTING "HARMONY"

During my twenty-year presidency at Fuller Seminary I made frequent visits to mainland China—at least once a year, for a total of twenty-nine visits. On one of those times in China I had a long discussion with a young government official at the State Administration for Religious Affairs. He told me that when he was first studying for government service, he was taught the official policy that religion was a bad thing and should ultimately be banished from Chinese culture. Then, when he entered government service, he said, that viewpoint was modified: the government decided that since they were not going to be able to ban religion effectively, they would have to find ways to tolerate it. More recently, he reported, there was a newer policy: the government realized that it needed to enlist religious groups as partners in actively promoting "social harmony." His observation explained for me some of the background to the decision that had been made by the 17th National Congress of the Communist Party of China in 2007, where the officials called for religious groups "to actively participate in building up a harmonious society."[4]

While recent reports out of China suggest that the government has stepped back from its more positive attitude toward faith communities, at the time I was glad to hear about the "social harmony" outlook. The word for "harmony" in Chinese has a Confucian connotation. A harmonious society is one in which each person knows how he or she fits into the larger social order and is motivated by a desire to function properly within that place in the scheme of things. For classic Confucianism, the sense of one's place was understood in terms of a rather rigid class structure. One is born into a certain social status and must learn to be content there. The adoption of "harmony" by the Chinese Communist Party was re-worked in terms of Marxist-type categories. But even though I did not like all that was associated in China with the idea of harmony, as understood by either Confucians or Communists, I thought that Christians could make good use of the idea in their public witness.

Not long after my conversation with the government official I was invited to give some talks to a hundred or so "registered church" pastors at a continuing education gathering held in the western part of China. The group had been polled ahead of time about topics they wanted to explore, and questions about how to be Christian citizens in China were high on the list submitted to me. I focused on several of the biblical passages I have already discussed here dealing with Peter's instruction to "submit" to government authority, with a special emphasis on Jeremiah's message to the exiles in Babylon and the apostle Peter's call to honor both government leaders and fellow citizens (1 Peter 2:13-17; Jeremiah 29:7).

I explained to the pastors that there was a positive link between the government's willingness to partner with churches for promoting social harmony and the prophet's mandate to the Babylonian exiles to see the shalom of the city where the Lord had placed them. While there would be some obvious differences between the government's vision of a harmonious society and the Christian commitment to shalom, there was also some overlap, and I urged them to seek out issues of common cause.

I reminded the pastors of the ways that the Christian community had quickly stepped in to serve victims of the 2008 earthquake—8.0 on the Richter scale—in the Sichuan region. The government had commended the churches for this effort. This kind cooperative initiative, I said, could serve as an excellent opportunity for Christian witness. Government-sponsored social services in China have been slow to find ways of addressing new realities—abandoned children, weakening of the traditional kinship system in caring for the elderly, growing addiction patterns, rural poor migrating to urban centers in search of employment—and the Christian community, in addressing these realities, can bear testimony to God's concern for orphans, widows, the poor, and the oppressed.

Here is my point in raising this Chinese example. It is certainly possible to question the motivations of the Chinese government in calling for the promotion of social harmony. And even apart from that, there clearly are differences between a robust biblical understanding of shalom and the party's appropriation of the Confucian notion of how everyone properly fits into the larger scheme of things. However, the invitation for religious groups to work alongside others in working for social harmony does offer an opportunity for Christians to make an effort to find ways to work for the well-being of the whole.

For Chinese Christians, then, however they might understand the government's motives in inviting religious groups to work for social harmony, or however they might interpret the meaning of a term that originated with Confucianism and was now being used by Communist Party leadership, the simple fact is that the opportunity was there as a matter of public record. The challenge was for Christians to respond by seeing the call to working for harmony as an opportunity to obey God's call to promote shalom.

We can say the same thing about American civil religion. Legitimate concerns can be raised about the uses to which religious language are sometimes put in the public arena, which means that we must think carefully about how we as Christians understand the theological meaning of that language. But the fact is that civil religion is there—with a long history of shaping how American citizens see their country's origin and destiny. The question is whether we take this reality as a positive challenge to put civil religion to good uses.

THE POSITIVE CASE

Here I need to get into a little bit of the scholarly discussion by reporting on an essay that has helped me to understand the positive role that civil religion can play in American public life. The essay titled "Civil Religion in America" was written in the 1960s by Robert Bellah, a sociologist at the University of California, Berkeley.[5] I read his essay when I first started my teaching career, but when I got to know him personally later in my career, I discovered him to be a devout Christian who was active in his local Episcopal congregation.

Bellah was a strong advocate of our democratic republic form of government. He liked the give-and-take character of our political system. People can be elected to office, and if they do not meet their constituents' expectations, they can be defeated in the next round of elections. Laws and policies can be put into effect, but they can be challenged and changed. What happens in our political life does not have to be seen as final.

Bellah liked all of that, but he was also convinced that there are standards of truth and justice that transcend existing policies. What we human beings set in place in configuring our life together can be misguided, even horribly so on occasion. Just because laws and practices have strong public support does not make them right. Ultimately, right has to be decided with reference to standards and ideals that are beyond the ebb and flow of popular opinion. We need to be periodically reminded of that, Bellah argued, and this is where civil religion enters into the picture. Religious ideas must never be used simply to baptize the status quo. Rather, they must serve to point us beyond the status quo to what ultimately matters for our collective life.

To make his point, Bellah offers historical examples of civil religion performing its proper role, typically on major national occasions—presidential inaugurations, special days of commemoration, moments of historical decisions, and national crises. These events are opportunities to look beyond the realities of political life to a point of view that is not merely a product of our own human designs.

In his essay Bellah used what was then a relatively recent national event to illustrate his point. He noted that in the late John F. Kennedy's inaugural address, delivered six years earlier, the newly elected president included three prominent references to God in his speech. The first was in his second sentence: "For I have sworn before you and Almighty God the same solemn oath our forbears prescribed nearly a century and three-quarters ago." Shortly after that, he observed "that the rights of man come not from the generosity of the state but from the hand of God." And Kennedy concluded his address with this call: "let us go forth to lead the land we love, asking His blessing and His help, but knowing that here on earth God's work must truly be our own."[6] These references to God, Bellah argued, are not merely sentimental. Nor should we be cynical about Kennedy's intent. In Kennedy's case it was a recognition of the importance of affirming at the beginning of his presidency "the religious legitimation of the highest political authority."[7]

Bellah also pointed to another presidential address, this one delivered by President Lyndon Johnson to a joint session of Congress, on the evening of March 15, 1965. His topic on that occasion was the Voting Rights Act that the legislators had just passed. At a dramatic moment in his speech, Johnson pointed out that above the pyramid on the great seal of the United States is a Latin phrase that proclaims, "He has favored our undertaking." The president observed that "God will not favor everything that we do. It is rather our duty to divine His will." Then he made this memorable declaration: "I cannot help believing that He truly favors the undertaking that we begin here tonight."[8]

Obviously, Kennedy's and Johnson's words are fairly generic religiously. If I were to fill my evangelical theological content into those presidential speeches, I would discuss sin, redemption, the need to honor the Bible's authority, and so on. But like Bellah I am not troubled that those convictions are not spelled out. They would have been out of place in a presidential inaugural address. What was not out of place was the insistence by each of them that above the ever-changing tides of public opinion there is a God who holds us as a people accountable to the standards of a "righteousness [that] exalts a nation" (Proverbs 14:34).

The idea of transcendence was central to Bellah's case. There is a court of opinion beyond the status quo with reference to which we must evaluate the way things are. We can see this notion operating in very ordinary parent-child relations. The mother says, "It's time for you to go to bed so quit playing and get your pajamas on!" The child: "I don't want to go to bed. Why do I have to?" Mother: "Because I'm your mother and I said so!" Child: "Why do I have to do it just because you say so? It's just not fair!"

In this very ordinary type of exchange, the child is appealing beyond the value statements of the status quo. Mommy may say so, but does that make it right? If the conversation were to continue, it would require claims about what is healthy for children, why authority patterns in a household are necessary, and so on.

Presidents Kennedy and Johnson were making that kind of case regarding our national life. This is what we are doing as a nation—but is it in accordance with God's standards? We have passed this legislation, but is it what God wills for human well-being?

There are those of our fellow citizens who understandably oppose bringing the divine into the picture. They do not acknowledge the existence of God. But Bellah was not ready to give into this dissent. Christians and other believers in a divinely ordained order can accept the presidential claims as stated, each of us reading our own theological content into them. Unbelievers will, admittedly, have to work a little harder—understanding "God's work" in terms of "the right kind of work." And this is what happened during the civil rights movement, when many nonreligious folks supported Martin Luther King Jr.'s appeals to the will of God in terms of claims that simply made reference to "justice." In advocating religious language, Bellah was taking advantage of the presence of a civil religion that has played a crucial role in our history—beginning with references to the will of the Creator in our founding documents.

OUR NATIONAL STORY

That acknowledgment of our history is another crucial factor in understanding a positive role for civil religion. Religious categories have long provided the framework for understanding the American nation's origins and destiny. Historians have pointed out, of course, that many of the founders of the American system were not orthodox Christians. Jefferson, Franklin, and others had deist views—

they acknowledged that a Creator got things started, but the deity was not for them the loving personal God of our biblical faith. But they were not reluctant to use explicit God-language in what they said about our founding principles.

In recent years objections to civil religious language have focused on how we frequently tell the story of our national beginnings and of our mission in the world. Many critics of civil religion have pointed to the ways in which people have used biblical images to offer a whitewashed story of our history. One standard study of religious influences in America is titled *Errand into the Wilderness*, an allusion to the biblical account of the travels of the children of Israel's pilgrimage in search of the Promised Land, with results that were destructive of the Native communities who were already here.[9]

The critics make an important point. The idea of a group of people going into the wilderness to create a new kind of nation provides a story of a nation's founding that can easily be used to hide some inconvenient facts by people who want to celebrate what they see as their country's unique calling. As I pointed out earlier, this was certainly the case with the narrative that was constructed by the Afrikaner community in South Africa. They saw their history as that of a freedom-loving, God-fearing people who were sent by the Lord from Europe into the wilderness of Africa's "Dark Continent." Those Dutch Calvinists explicitly appealed to conditions set by the prophet Joshua when the Israelites settled into the Promised Land. The original inhabitants would still be allowed to live there, Joshua stipulated, but now as "bondmen" who would serve the Israelites as their "hewers of wood and drawers of water" (Joshua 9:23 KJV).

That way of telling a story about national origins also shows up in our own narratives about America's beginnings. The slavery system also, as is well known, was defended by claiming biblical justifications.

An honest awareness of that history should be sufficient to make us wary of using religious categories for shaping our national stories. Except for one thing however: different uses of civil religion have played a key role in finding measures to correct the patterns of injustice. Black Christians in South Africa and the United States, seeing themselves in a situation much like the Israelites enslaved in Egypt, cried out to the pharaohs of racism, "Let my people go!"

I have already pointed to Martin Luther King Jr.'s gifts in framing his prophetic message in the terminology of civil religion. His oft-quoted "I Have a Dream" speech is a powerful example of this skill. Here, for example, is his brilliant use of a passage from Isaiah 40, followed by a refrain from "America":

I have a dream that one day every valley shall be exalted, every hill and mountain shall be made low, the rough places shall be made plain, and the crooked places shall be made straight and the glory of the Lord will be revealed and all flesh shall see it together. . . .

This will be the day when all of God's children will be able to sing with a new meaning—"my country, 'tis of thee; sweet land of liberty; of thee I sing; land where my fathers died, land of the pilgrim's pride; from every mountainside, let freedom ring"—and if America is to be a great nation, this must become true.

So let freedom ring from the prodigious hilltops

of New Hampshire.

Let freedom ring from the mighty mountains
　　of New York.

Let freedom ring from the heightening Alleghenies
　　of Pennsylvania.

Let freedom ring from the snow-capped Rockies
　　of Colorado.

Let freedom ring from the curvaceous slopes
　　of California.

But not only that.

Let freedom ring from Stone Mountain of Georgia.

Let freedom ring from Lookout Mountain
　　of Tennessee.

Let freedom ring from every hill and molehill
　　of Mississippi, from every mountainside,
　　let freedom ring.[10]

A "USABLE" RELIGION

Dr. King's declaration that committing to racial justice will allow American citizens to sing a traditional patriotic song "with a new meaning" is an encouraging word for those of us who strive for an honest patriotic love for our nation. We can see the misdeeds and hypocrisies of our collective past, but we are not required thereby to start all over again in thinking about our past, present, and future. We can draw on the civil religious resources that are already ours to arrive at some new understandings and insights. We can expand beyond the limits of our past grasp of who is included in the *all* when we confess in words from the Declaration of Independence that "all men are created equal, that they are endowed by their Creator with certain unalienable Rights." We can find new ways to promote laws and practices that "make our land be bright with freedom's holy light."[11]

This requires, of course, the hard—and sometimes painful—work of looking honestly at our past. But as the historian Jill Lepore has observed, while "writing national history creates plenty of problems . . . , not writing national history creates more problems, and those problems are worse."[12]

Again, civil religion—including the variety set forth so compellingly by Martin Luther King Jr.—falls significantly short of the full content of a robust biblical orthodoxy. However, what is included in civil religion allows us to join with others in envisioning what Bellah describes as a "transcendent goal for the political process" that enables us to reflect on our collective American experience in a larger perspective than the day-to-day preoccupations of ordinary politics.[13]

Civil religion at its best also points us to future possibilities for correcting the mistakes of our past and present. It can inspire us to refuse to be locked into the practices and interpretations that have sometimes given us a restricted understanding of our national identity. Our expanded sense of the "all men" of our Declaration of Independence frees us up to listen to voices that we have long ignored, as well as to new voices that we should be welcoming into our national conversation. And the convictions that many of us hold that ground the beliefs of civil religion in a deeper biblical faith can serve as our motivation to engage in this broad conversation with confidence that God will bless our efforts.

Here is a question that is often asked by Christians who are critical of any embrace of civil religion: Is it pleasing to God for us to be willing to use religion to foster a sense of national unity? That is always a good question to ask, especially given the examples of thinkers like Plato and Rousseau who encourage authorities to speak in religious language simply because doing so is useful in promoting certain political goals.

That approach is a perversion of religious convictions. Our task is to make proper use of the expressions associated with civil religion in our efforts to obey the revealed will of the Lord who calls us to serve him in our active engagements with the larger human community:

> He has shown you, O mortal, what is good.
> And what does the LORD require of you?
> To act justly and to love mercy
> and to walk humbly with your God. (Micah 6:8)

One important function of civil religion is to promote national unity. Admittedly, national unity can be invoked to serve bad purposes. It can be used to encourage hostility toward other nations, and domestically it can be a means of marginalizing groups that are not seen as belonging to the real "us." But it can also reinforce our awareness that everyone in our nation is created in the divine image, whether or not they share our Christian convictions.

SOLEMN "SWEARING"

One element that I find significant in Robert Bellah's case for a healthy version of civil religion is his focus on the role of religious themes in major national ceremonial events—as in his discussion of presidential inaugural addresses. Some related examples may not be as "officially" ceremonial, but they have come to gain that kind of status, as in Abraham Lincoln's

Gettysburg Address, Lyndon Johnson's congressional re-
marks on the voting rights legislation, and Martin Luther
King Jr.'s great Lincoln Memorial oration.

There are other more frequent civil religious expressions, of
course: the "under God" clause in the Pledge of Allegiance,
and lines in "God Bless America" and other patriotic songs.
But the general point that Bellah is emphasizing is that a
properly functioning civil religion should not take the form of
extensive theological discourses in our public lives. They are
reminders of what we might think of as significant *reminders
of transcendence*, serving the purpose of keeping us aware that
there is more to our civic engagement than the ebb and flow
of popular opinion and practical political strategizing.

We see this same kind of influence at work in the British
context, where there is very little talk about religion in day-
to-day politics. The story has been told that when Tony Blair
was prime minister, some of his aides discouraged him from
saying things about how his Catholic convictions related to
his policy views. They were reported to have said that in
British politics "we don't do God." My own view is that rightly
understood their observation makes sense—even though
they could have put their point in a less dismissive tone. In a
pluralistic society we must focus on formulating policies and
practices in terms that will be compelling to diverse constitu-
encies. In British life, however, Queen Elizabeth has had a
different role. In her annual talks to the nation she has typically spoken in very personal terms about her trust in God's
purposes in her own life and in the life of the nation. In doing
so she is employing civil religion themes in a manner that fits
well with a Bellah-type perspective.

None of this means that extensive theological teaching about faith and public life is inappropriate in other contexts. Indeed, in our Christian communities such teaching has been sadly lacking. But that much-needed teaching must include instructing us in how to think about the issues of public life while also equipping us to make our case in acceptably effective ways in the public arena.

While I will not take on this big topic here, I do want to emphasize the importance of selective and faithful uses of oaths and pledges in public life. In citing President Kennedy's inaugural address, for example, Bellah quotes him as saying, "For I have sworn before you and Almighty God the same solemn oath our forebears prescribed nearly a century and three-quarters ago."[14] This "swearing" before God is highly appropriate on such an important national occasion. But it would not be a good thing for a president to engage in a similar kind of "swearing" in regular press conferences. When my wife, Phyllis, and I were married over a half century ago we made solemn vows—in effect, oaths—to each other in the presence of God. But it would not be appropriate for either of us to make a promise to each other about a daily task by adding the clause "God helping me."

Again, this topic of solemn swearing is a large and complex subject. Some Christian groups—Quakers and Mennonites, for example—believe that the taking of "oaths" as such is forbidden by Scripture. I adhere to the more mainstream Christian view that solemn vows and pledges are legitimate if we are intentional and discerning in how we fit them into our lives. Jesus tells us to "let your 'Yes' be 'Yes,' and your 'No,' 'No'" (Matthew 5:37 NKJV)—that should be enough, he assures us, for any faithful disciple. But on public occasions, as in swearing in court "to tell the truth . . . so help me God," or in making vows in the wedding ceremonies, we can see ourselves as bearing witness to the larger human community that we believe that standards of truthfulness, pursuing justice, and being faithful to our promises are not products of human design, but point to the "beyond" and "above" of our creaturely lives.

PUTTING IT IN PRACTICE

I have had pastors contact me about invitations they receive to pray, for example, at a city council meeting. One of them said that he had no desire to offer a "civil religion kind of prayer" so he was wondering whether he should just politely turn the invitation down or "give them a real Christian prayer!" In a phone conversation I reminded him that there are thousands of chaplains in the military, prisons, hospitals, and other nonsectarian settings who share that pastor's strong Christian convictions while doing on a regular basis what he was being asked to do as a one-time assignment.

I have taught courses on several occasions for chaplains serving in the military—including one two-week stint on a Navy base—and I have been impressed by the creative ways they make use of complex challenges that they face in their ministries. I have heard their expressions of frustration and hurt over how they are misunderstood by many of their fellow clergy who see them as "watering down" the Christian message, and in some cases by those who consider their ministries as "selling out to American militarism." On the military side there are officials who see them as outsiders to the military system.

To put it bluntly, these persons are genuinely Christian practitioners of "civil religion" on a daily basis. They recognize both the opportunities and the limitations presented by conforming to nonsectarian religious standards as they seek to honor their calling from God in situations of genuine human need. Their efforts—laudable ones, I want to insist—must also be taken into account in assessing the overall strengths and defects of American civil religion.

"WHILE WE STILL CAN"

I have good arguments with Christian friends who disagree with me about the positive role that civil religion plays in our national life. One question I regularly pursue with them is whether they believe we would really be better off if we simply banned all references to God and the like in our public discourse. This is not a hypothetical question. Persons of no religious belief at all frequently complain about "God and country" talk these days, and it is not unthinkable that organized efforts to get rid of the language of civil religion will start to grow. The mere possibility of that happening is at least a good way for us to think about the role of civil religion in promoting the health of our society.

For me, I am comforted by the fact that civil religion is still with us. As I have been writing this chapter, the current president publicly expressed sympathy for a family experiencing a tragic loss, telling them that "I am praying for you." Daily prayers are offered at the opening of sessions of the US Senate. We still sing about sacred matters at civic gatherings. Schoolchildren pledge allegiance to a nation "under God." I certainly wish for more to be said in those contexts than the guidelines regulating the public use of religious concepts will allow, but I do not want less. For those of us who both fear God and love our country, not everything associated with generic "God and country" themes can be seen as misguided.

NINE

HOPES AND FEARS

At several points thus far I have paid attention to lines from songs—ones that we sing in church and at civic gatherings. Now one more: a line from the Christmas carol "O Little Town of Bethlehem." I quote it frequently in speeches, sermons, and my writings: "The hopes and fears of all the years are met in Thee tonight."[1]

The profundity of that line hit me when, a couple of decades ago, I was walking through a Michigan mall, surrounded by people doing their Christmas shopping. I was stopped in my tracks when I heard the recorded voice of Perry Como singing those words over the sound system. It struck me that much of what was going on around me was about hopes and fears. And not just surface ones, as in "I hope I can get out of here in time to pick Freda up at school," or "I'm afraid that the sweater I just bought for Archie is the wrong size." Deeper hopes and fears that drive our thoughts and actions: the hopes for security and safety, the fears of rejection and loss.

Those kinds of hopes and fears are also present in other public places: legislatures, voting booths, campaign rallies, and lines of folks waiting to be served at the local post office.

I find this helpful in thinking about what is going on when we angrily quarrel over issues of public life. I draw a parallel to lovers' quarrels. A couple has an angry exchange about some practical issue, and it heats up to the point where they get into accusations and name-calling. They cut it off finally by stomping away. Each of them is thinking that, given the things that were said, the relationship has to be over. After a while, though, one of them approaches the other and asks in a soft pleading voice, "Can we talk?" Then, "I'm so sorry about what I said. I really didn't mean those things! What I was really trying to tell you was . . ." And now the conversation is framed in terms of hopes and fears.

When I talked to a church group during the 2000 presidential campaign, I used that story as an entry point into seeing much of our political quarreling as really motivated by hopes and fears. This means, I said, that we do well to get beyond labeling and attributing motives to folks we disagree with. It is wrong simply to define our fellow human beings in terms of, for example, how they vote.

In the discussion period after my talk, a young woman spoke up about her serious political disagreements with her fellow church members. As a racial minority member of the congregation, she said she was often so angry that she had bad thoughts about them and even wanted to call them names to their faces. She had even thought seriously about joining another church. "But now," she said in a soft voice, "I just want to ask you for something." She paused, and then in a barely audible voice: "Can we *talk*?" She had not only gotten the point of what I had been saying, but she deepened my own understanding of the point.

INNER PATRIOTISM

Introducing the relevance of hopes and fears as I near the end of my explorations here fits well with what I have been focusing on all along. I have made much of the subjective in discussing patriotism. I have emphasized affection, love, and honoring. These are all states of inner *feeling*, and now I want to continue with yet one more inner disposition: *compassion*. The link between patriotism and *compassion* was made by one of my favorite authors, and to explain why I find her so helpful on this subject, I must provide some biographical detail about her personal wrestlings with patriotism.

Simone Weil was born into a Jewish family in France in 1909, and she died at the age of thirty-four in 1943. Weil's parents were professed agnostics, and she continued that family commitment to unbelief as she became a respected scholar with strong Marxist sympathies. Her life changed dramatically, however, when seven years before her death while reading a poem that a Christian friend had recommended to her, suddenly "Christ himself came down and took possession of me."[2] This experience completely transformed her views about life, including her perspective on society and politics. This did not mean for her that she had to give up her political activism though. In her final years she passionately engaged in the French Resistance against the Nazi scourge.

Weil thought much about her relationship as a Christian to the French nation, and she wrote a book on the subject during her final years. The title she chose is telling: *The Need for Roots*. She wanted to have a sense of being rooted in a French identity while at the same time having many strong criticisms of her homeland.

Her criticisms of France were certainly well founded. As she was writing about rootedness, terrible things were happening there. Not only were the Nazis in control of the country, but the French authorities had willingly entered into a pact with Germany, welcoming the occupying troops. Furthermore, this willingness to collaborate with Hitler's minions was shared by many French citizens, some of whom eagerly befriended the Nazis. Indeed, French people frequently helped the Germans round up Jews for transportation to death camps, and some young French men even volunteered as soldiers in the German military.

Weil found all of that deeply distressing. She was Jewish by birth, and she sustained a deep love for her fellow Jews. But she also struggled to understand her bonds to all the citizens of the land of her birth. She genuinely wanted to find the proper way to love the French nation. She wanted a patriotism that could give her a strong sense of being rooted.

In her search for the right way to love her country, Weil made use of a distinction that has come to mean much to me. She rejected the kind of patriotism that she labeled as "a patriotism founded upon pride and pomp-and-glory." Instead, she wrote, she wanted to cultivate a patriotism that is "inspired by compassion."[3]

CULTIVATING PATRIOTIC COMPASSION

It is important to emphasize that Weil's compassion for her country was *informed*. Being possessed by Christ changed her thinking about her relationship to France. Having given much attention to the affective here, this knowing part of the picture needs to be stressed. Our feelings toward our nation cannot simply be free-floating. They must be solidly grounded in an honest grasp of the *facts* about the nation. Clearly, as a Jew wanting to love a France that was collaborating with Nazism, Weil had to face up to some painful realities, which in turn led her to engage in supporting the dangerous underground efforts. She saw the flaws of her nation and supported difficult remedial strategies.

My guess is that the claim that America as a nation has real flaws would be agreed upon by just about everyone. That does not mean, though, that we agree on what the flaws are or how to rank the ones we do agree on. In exploring our disagreements, we need reference points beyond our individual subjective preferences. That was the lesson that Robert Bellah insisted on in his important discussion of civil religion. We need those occasions, he observed—national holidays, presidential inaugurations—when we remind ourselves as a people that patriotism is not only about power politics or the ebb and flow of popular opinion or power politics. Our national conversation has to take place with a recognition of ideals and values that are not of our own human making.[4]

We must continually remain aware of what was declared at the American nation's founding, as we presented to the world our Declaration of Independence: "We hold these truths . . ." These are the transcendent reference points that are always relevant to any conversation about who we are as a people and where we are going.

BEING ROOTED

Simone Weil wanted a love of country that had deep roots in a sense of *belonging*. She came to experience that belonging, that rootedness in French peoplehood, by being open to feeling genuine pain on behalf of her country. She realized that the love of nation will often bring *sadness* to our souls.

That being patriotic might bring genuine sadness into our lives should not surprise us. We can see this by thinking about how the capacity for sadness is a key element in our love of our families. If having a loving relationship with my kinfolk can only be sustained by my being proud of them, or by my needing the stimulus of family celebrations, then my sense of belonging does not go deep. To be sure, being proud of the accomplishments of people we love and enjoying family gatherings are good things. But being a healthy family member also means hanging in there with loved ones even when they bring me grief. Sadness is a necessary element in compassion. Some people treat empathy and compassion as close in meaning, but empathy covers more inner territory than compassion. I can have empathy for people experiencing joy as well as for people experiencing sadness. But compassion is only appropriate when things have gone wrong.

Simone Weil experienced her love for France by feeling sad about what her country was going through. There was little cause for joy at that time in France's history, but in linking patriotism to sadness she was making a more general point. Even in what we might think of as the best of times, nations are held together by fragile bonds. Our life together is always a mixture of collective hopes and fears.

Weil sums it up nicely in this comment: to see her country as "something beautiful and precious," she says, means seeing it as "in the first place, imperfect, and secondly, very frail and liable to suffer misfortune." It is precisely these features that made being French something that she experienced as "necessary to cherish and preserve."[5]

Those words capture my own experience of being an American. My country also falls far short of perfection, plagued by frailty and frequently touched by misfortune. But I also see in the United States something of a beauty that I find endearing, and I want to love America, not because it is the greatest nation in the world but because it is *my* country, the place where the Lord has placed me. To say that I love my mother in a different way than I could possibly love your mother is not to make a grandiose claim about the person who birthed me. It is simply to accept the particularity of my own place in the world. It is to have identified my own roots.

Healthy roots go deep. And to experience rootedness in our national traditions and ideals takes extra work these days. Commentators on our "postmodern" culture often characterize our contemporary lives as too much on the surfaces of reality. We do a lot of surfing and scrolling on our tech devices. People talk with enthusiasm about temporarily hooking up. We pursue our daily schedules at a fast pace. Geographic mobility has meant being separated by significant distances from extended family. We even sometimes shop around for a congregation to join.

When we simply give in to all of this, we can become fragmented selves. Albert Borgmann, a philosopher who has written much about the effects of new technologies on present-day life, puts it nicely when he says that when we spend so much time on "surfaces," we fail to maintain an awareness of "the eloquence of things" in their particularity."[6] In not allowing her relationship to France to be reduced to a superficial "patriotism founded upon pride and pomp-and-glory," Simone Weil discovered an eloquence in her national identity—a fragile eloquence to be sure, but something that deserved to be nurtured and cherished.

President Kennedy's inspired words again: "Here on earth God's work must truly be our own."[7] The word *work* there is highly appropriate. It does not come easily. The necessary work is much needed in our era. Diverse lifestyles, races, religions, classes, ideologies, and partisan conflicts threaten to weaken the social bond to the breaking point. The only real remedy is the one Dr. King preached about in his sermon about loving our enemies. When we allow God's love to permeate our consciousness of human nature, he said, "You begin to love men, not because they are likable, but because God loves them. You look at every man, and you love him because you know God loves him. And he might be the worst person you've ever seen."[8] We saw John Calvin making the same point when he insisted that we have to work at seeing people, even folks who for us are quite unlikable, as they are "contemplated in God, not in themselves."[9]

Mother Teresa did not like to be thought of as an activist. When people would call her that, she would correct them. The community that she founded, the Missionaries of Charity, is actually a "contemplative" order she would say. She and her Sisters would spend hours reading the Gospel stories about Jesus and experiencing his presence in worship. Then they were prepared to go out onto the streets of Calcutta, looking for him in his "distressing disguise" among the poorest of the poor.[10]

KEEP WRESTLING

I have a somewhat different theology from that of Mother Teresa, but I do like her profound notion of public activity grounded in contemplation. I began my discussion saying that I was not going to give how-to advice about being patriotic but that I wanted to invite fellow believers to wrestle with me on the challenges of citizenship. It has not been possible to talk about my own wrestling without showing my hand on some political specifics. But when, for example, I have raised admittedly controversial issues about the scope of government, I have mainly wanted to encourage engaging in informed arguments with reference to actual issues. As I conclude, I will get preachy, though, by offering four guidelines for how to keep at the wrestling—guidelines that I think ought to inform all of us, regardless of our differences on political specifics.

First guideline: *do the work of contemplation*. Go beyond the surfaces in seeing others, especially others whom we might quite naturally dislike. When Mother Teresa talked about seeing Jesus in his "distressing disguise" among the dying lepers whom she served on the streets of Calcutta, she obviously had in mind that teaching of Jesus where the Savior tells of a day when he will reward those who ministered to him when he was hungry, thirsty, naked, and imprisoned. Righteous people will ask him, he says, when they saw him in these situations. And Jesus will answer that when they did it to the least of human beings in need, they did it to him (Matthew 25:34-46). The kind of contemplation that Mother Teresa had in mind—as did Dr. King and John Calvin—enables righteous people to engage in a special kind of seeing.

That way of seeing takes work, especially since in public life it often goes counter to the way we want to see things. Furthermore, since issues of citizenship often mean disagreements with those we are being called to see, our contemplation will also necessitate listening to stories as well.

Second guideline: *cultivate compassion*. The kinds of cases that Jesus mentioned—hunger, thirst, lack of proper clothing, the forsakenness of being in prison—are, to say the least, sad conditions. The people served by the Sisters in Calcutta often experienced these conditions in the extreme. When coming upon a leper who lies dying in a filthy gutter, all they can do is whisper words of love into the person's ear. It is not likely that we will be called to that sort of desperate situation on the American political scene, but there may be times when we will hear stories of injustice and oppression to which our only response can be to utter whispers of love. We need to prepare for those encounters by nurturing the ability to express social, political, and economic compassion.

Third guideline: *go deep in the quest for rootedness*. Simone Weil was searching for her French roots in full awareness that she was already deeply rooted in her faith. Her identity in Christ was for her rock solid. And we must see our own rootedness in the same way. That we are citizens of the United States is certainly relevant for who we understand ourselves to be. God calls us to love the country of our citizenship, caring in profound ways about its shalom. But that identity does not define us in the deepest places of our being. Like Simone Weil, we must see ourselves as fully possessed by Jesus Christ, as believers who are brothers and sisters from the tribes and nations of the earth—

citizens with them in his kingdom. Nothing else can rival those allegiances.

And the fourth guideline: *trust Jesus*. He not only came to address "the hopes and fears of all the years," as we sing in the carol "O Little Town of Bethlehem."[11] He took them into his very person. The writer of Hebrews expresses this clearly: "For we do not have a high priest who is unable to empathize with our weaknesses, but we have one who has been tempted in every way, just as we are—yet he did not sin" (Hebrews 4:15). That he took all of that to the manger of Bethlehem and then to the cross of Calvary means that we can face our fears because he also speaks to the deepest hopes of the human spirit. The God who sheds his grace on each of us individually sent his Son into the world to take on the hopes and fears of *all* the years, including the collective hopes and fears of nations and peoples. To be assured of that in the deep places of our hearts is what should inspire us to keep wrestling with what it means to be patriotic Christians.

ACKNOWLEDGMENTS

Much of what I discuss in these pages is the product of a half century of teaching on issues of faith and politics. More precisely, it results from what I have *been taught* by the students in my classes, as well as by many friends with whom I have had countless dialogues—yes, and even some passionate arguments—about matters of Christian citizenship.

I began writing this book in 2020 when I joined the staff of the Paul B. Henry Institute for the Study of Christianity and Politics at Calvin University as senior research fellow. Paul Henry was my former colleague and good friend, who served for eight years with distinction as a Republican member of Congress, until his untimely death in 1993. Paul's accomplishments as a Christian who was deeply committed to working for the common good were very much on my mind as I explored the topics I write about in these pages.

I am grateful for helpful comments on drafts of various chapters, from Micah Watson, Heather Kaemingk, Al Hsu, and an anonymous reader at InterVarsity Press. I am particularly grateful to my gifted student research assistant at Calvin, Lauren Baas, who offered key insights all along the way. I look forward to the brilliant books that she will someday be writing on Christian political thought.

NOTES

1. WRESTLING TOGETHER

[1]Heidelberg Catechism, Question and Answer 1, www.ccel.org/creeds/heidelberg -cat.html.

[2]William James, *The Varieties of Religious Experience* (New York: Longmans, Green and Company, 1917), vi.

[3]Phillips Brooks, "O Little Town of Bethlehem," 1868.

[4]Irving Berlin, "God Bless America," 1918.

[5]James Baldwin, *Notes of a Native Son* (Boston: Beacon Press, 2012), 9.

[6]Martin Luther King Jr., *Letter from Birmingham Jail* (New York: Penguin Books, 2018), 26.

2. "WE THE PEOPLE"

[1]Joseph Medicott Scriven, "What a Friend We Have in Jesus," 1855.

[2]"Away in a Manger," 1882.

[3]Katharine Lee Bates, "America the Beautiful," 1895.

[4]Samuel Francis Smith, "America (My Country, 'Tis of Thee)," 1831.

[5]Francis Scott Key, "The Star-Spangled Banner," 1814.

[6]Smith, "America."

[7]Bates, "America the Beautiful."

[8]Smith, "America."

[9]Abraham Lincoln, "The Gettysburg Address," https://rmc.library.cornell.edu /gettysburg/good_cause/transcript.htm.

[10]George E. Reedy, *The Twilight of the Presidency* (New York: Signet, 1971).

[11]Aristotle, *Nicomachean Ethics*, book 8, http://classics.mit.edu/Aristotle /nicomachaen.8.viii.html.

[12]A version of this section originally appeared in a short online piece I wrote for the *Christian Post*: "Former Fuller President: Boy Scouts Helped Me. Who Will Fill Civic Hole?" February 28, 2020, www.christianpost.com/voices/former -fuller-president-boy-scouts-helped-me-who-will-fill-civic-hole.html.

[13]"About the BSA," Boy Scouts of America, www.scouting.org/about/.

[14]Ronald Thiemann, *Constructing a Public Theology: The Church in a Pluralistic Culture* (Louisville, KY: Westminster John Knox), 43.

[15]Jill Lepore, *This America: The Case for the Nation* (New York: Liveright, 2019), 22-23.

3. HUMAN BONDS

[1]Robert D. Putnam, *Bowling Alone: The Collapse and Revival of American Community* (New York: Simon & Schuster, 2000), 28.

[2]Thomas Hobbes, "Of the Causes, Generation, and Definition of a Common-Wealth," in *Leviathan*, part 2, chap. 17, www.gutenberg.org/files/3207/3207-h/3207-h.htm.

[3]This formula, cited by Plato, Aristotle, and many others, is seen as originating in Caesar Flavius Justinian's *The Institutes of Justinian*, where the first line of book 1, title 1 is "Justice is the set and constant purpose which gives to every man his due."

[4]Irving Berlin, "God Bless America," 1918.

[5]John Calvin, *Institutes of the Christian Religion*, ed. John T. McNeill, trans. Ford Lewis Battles (Philadelphia: Westminster Press, 1960), 2:8, 54-55, 417-19.

[6]Henri J. M. Nouwen, *The Genesee Diary: Report from a Trappist Monastery* (Garden City, NY: Doubleday, 1976), 74-75.

4. WHERE "HONOR IS DUE"

[1]Elvina Hall, "Jesus Paid It All," 1865.

[2]Joseph Medicott Scriven, "What a Friend We Have in Jesus," 1855.

5. THE SCOPE OF GOVERNMENT

[1]The well-known seventeenth century Scottish theologian Samuel Rutherford, in the twelfth article of his "A Defense of the Government of the Church of Scotland" (1642) writes, "The king bears the sword and is there as a politic president and nursing father."

[2]This section makes use of materials in my Religious News Service column "Government: Does Size Matter?" April 5, 2017, https://religionnews.com/2017/04/05/government-does-size-matter/.

6. LEARNING FROM ARGUMENTS

[1]José Míguez Bonino, *Christians and Marxists: The Mutual Challenge to Revolution* (Grand Rapids, MI: Eerdmans, 1976), 58.

[2]John Calvin, *Institutes of the Christian Religion*, ed. John T. McNeill, trans. Ford Lewis Battles (Philadelphia: Westminster Press, 1960), 2:3, 6, 273.

[3]Timothy Keller, "How Do Christians Fit into the Two-Party System? They Don't," *New York Times*, September 29, 2018, www.nytimes.com/2018/09/29/opinion/sunday/christians-politics-belief.html.

[4]Keller, "How Do Christians Fit?"

[5]G. K. Chesterton, "The Case Against Corruption," in *Autobiography* (London: Hutchinson, 1936), chap. 9, https://gutenberg.net.au/ebooks13/1301201h .html.

[6]Peter Raymond Scholtes, "They'll Know We Are Christians by Our Love," in *Hymnal for Young Christians*, ed. Robert Blue (Chicago: F. E. L. Pub., 1966).

[7]Charlotte Elliott, "Just as I Am," 1835.

7. PATRIOTISM IN CHURCH

[1]Samuel Francis Smith, "America (My Country, 'Tis of Thee)," 1831.

[2]Irving Berlin, "God Bless America," 1918.

[3]Katharine Lee Bates, "America the Beautiful," 1895.

[4]Bates, "America the Beautiful."

8. RELIGION IN PUBLIC LIFE?

[1]*The Federalist Papers*, selected and edited by Roy P. Fairfield (Garden City, NY: Anchor Books, 1961), 18-19.

[2]Plato, *The Republic*, book 3. Available in many editions. The classic translation by Benjamin Jowett is at www.gutenberg.org/files/1497/1497-h/1497-h.htm.

[3]Jean-Jacques Rousseau, *The Social Contract*, trans. Willmoore Kendall (Chicago: Henry Regnery Company, 1954), 160.

[4]Quoted in the editorial introduction, *Chinese Theological Review*, vol. 22 (2010), viii.

[5]Bellah's essay "Civil Religion in America" along with a number of critical responses to it, is published in Russell E. Richey and Donald G. Jones, eds., *American Civil Religion* (New York: Harper & Row, 1974), 21-44.

[6]Transcript of John F. Kennedy's Inaugural Address (1961), www.ourdocuments .gov/doc.php?flash=false&doc=91&page=transcript.

[7]Bellah, "Civil Religion in America," 24.

[8]President Lyndon B. Johnson's Speech to Congress on Voting Rights, March 15, 1965, RG 46, Records of the United States Senate, National Archives, www.archives.gov/legislative/features/voting-rights-1965/johnson.html.

[9]See Perry Miller, *Errand into the Wilderness* (1956; reprint, Cambridge, MA: Belknap, 1984).

[10]Martin Luther King Jr., *I Have a Dream: Writings and Speeches that Changed the World* (New York: Harper One, 1986), 105.

[11]Samuel Francis Smith, "America (My Country, 'Tis of Thee)," 1831.

[12] Jill Lepore, *This America: The Case for the Nation* (New York: Liveright, 2019), 132.

[13] Bellah, "Civil Religion in America."

[14] Bellah, "Civil Religion in America."

9. HOPES AND FEARS

[1] Phillips Brooks, "O Little Town of Bethlehem," 1868.

[2] Gene Veith provides a fine account of the circumstances of her conversion, as well as the poem that she was reading when it happened, in his blog posting, "The Conversion of Simone Weil," *Cranach: The Blog of Veith*, June 2, 2021, www.patheos.com/blogs/geneveith/2021/06/simone-weils-conversion/.

[3] Simone Weil, *The Need for Roots: Prelude to a Declaration of Duties Towards Mankind* (Paris: Gallimard, 1949; New York: Routledge, 2002), 174.

[4] Robert Bellah, "Civil Religion in America," in *American Civil Religion*, ed. Russell E. Richey and Donald G. Jones (New York: Harper & Row, 1974).

[5] Weil, *Need for Roots*, 175.

[6] Albert Borgmann, *Crossing the Postmodern Divide* (Chicago: University of Chicago Press, 1992), 51, 106.

[7] Transcript of John F. Kennedy's Inaugural Address (1961), www.ourdocuments.gov/doc.php?flash=false&doc=91&page=transcript.

[8] Martin Luther King Jr., "Loving Your Enemies," Sermon Delivered at Dexter Avenue Baptist Church, November 17, 1947, Martin Luther King, Jr., Research and Education Institute, Stanford University, https://kinginstitute.stanford.edu/king-papers/documents/loving-your-enemies-sermon-delivered-dexter-avenue-baptist-church.

[9] John Calvin, *Institutes of the Christian Religion*, ed. John T. McNeill, trans. Ford Lewis Battles (Philadelphia: Westminster Press, 1960), 2:8, 55, 219.

[10] Mother Teresa of Calcutta, *My Life for the Poor*, ed. José Luis González-Balada and Janet N. Playfoot (San Francisco: Harper & Row, 1985), 18.

[11] Brooks, "O Little Town of Bethlehem."

ALSO BY RICHARD J. MOUW

Uncommon Decency
978-0-8308-3309-2